THE TEN CRITICAL LAWS

OF

RELATIONSHIP

DR. ROBB THOMPSON

The Ten Critical Laws of Relationship
ISBN 1-889723-52-5
Copyright © 2005 by Robb Thompson
Family Harvest Church
18500 92nd Avenue
Tinley Park, Illinois 60477

Collaborative Development: Karen Jahn, Dr. Dennis D. Sempebwa
Editing: Karen Jahn
Design: Amanda Reeves

Contents

The Ten Critical Laws of Relationship

Relationships are immensely similar to banks—what you put in, is exactly what you can take out. However, when you apply these Ten Critical Laws, outlined masterfully by Dr. Robb Thompson, your personal account becomes interest bearing with no late fees. *The Ten Critical Laws of Relationship* provides Kingdom solutions and practical explanations for establishing Godly relationships for both men and women alike. You will see, your time invested in reading this outstanding literary work will yield large returns in your personal and professional relationships, but most of all with the fulfillment of your destiny.

Bishop Eddie L. Long
Senior Pastor, New Birth
Atlanta, Georgia

Dr. Robb Thompson has an understanding of why relationships break down and how they can either be protected or restored. I would recommend this book to anyone who wants to experience success with other people.

Dr. Bill Gothard
Founder and President
Institute In Basic Life Principles
Oak Brook, Illinois

Everyone who reads *The Ten Critical Laws of Relationship* will benefit and be inspired to examine both their motives and actions in all their relationships, but especially in those that are closest to them. This powerful treatise on interacting with others will help people understand the responsibility of present relationships, and weigh the cost of future ones, while refining the manner in which one treats others.

Tommy Barnett
Senior Pastor
Phoenix First Assembly of God
Phoenix, Arizona

The challenge of building long term mutually beneficial relationship crosses all cultural, sexual and age barriers, and now at last we have some usable, practicable principles that will reveal to us as we are, and show us how we can change for the better.

Reading through Dr. Robb Thompson's new book *The Ten Critical Laws of Relationship* will take you through a mental corridor of mirrors exposing every facet of avoidance, falsehood and weakness in your relationships, and then like a directional compass, point you toward a pathway of truth, kindness and confidence.

I recommend you read and study this fine work and enjoy the benefit that it will bring to you and those you want to relate to.

I wish I had this book 50 years ago.

Dr. Peter J. Daniels
International Business Statesman
Strathalbyn, Australia

Acknowledgments

I would like to acknowledge those who have been instrumental in this work being penned.

To my wife, Linda, whose strong leadership and nurturing skills have caused me to press hard into the unseen and bring back the principles that will promote even the most mediocre of men.

To my father, Peter Daniels, to whom I owe my entire identity and future. You have brought me to a place of believing that God can change the destiny of even the most destitute of men. You have validated me.

To Dr. Rick Renner, a friend who is touching the world but still has time to relate to me in an ever increasing way...Thank you.

To Dr. John Avanzini, who has been an example of ministry from the pastorate to the itinerate. He is the picture of character and understanding...Thank you.

To Dr. Mike Murdock, for your willingness to spend endless hours helping me to discover my assignment and distinction in this life. To you I owe my ability to peer into life and extract principles from its almost undetectable sources. This is a debt that could never be repaid. I will be forever grateful.

To Kevin Leary, whose friendship to me has never wavered, even in my most abandoned moments.

To my Pastoral Staff, whose willingness to listen has caused me to ask heaven for more understanding of human needs.

To Dr. Dennis Sempebwa and Karen Jahn, whose consistent editing, encouragement and desire to complete has put this work in your hands.

Lastly, I would like to thank my enemies, for without you I would be a man without a future.

Dr. Robert Daniels Thompson

I would like to dedicate this book

to all the unattached who desire relationships

that will unlock the rusted doors of their lives

and create a new future.

May divine providence stop the hands of time,

in order to alter the course of history

by providing those most necessary companions,

who will become the Golden Links to an Abundant Future...

Dr. Robert Daniels Thompson

Every Relationship Contains Rules.

Those rules are unspoken, undocumented, and varied. The rules must be discerned, respected, and honored for the relationship to have impartation, longevity, or the strength to withstand seasons of adversity.

Every uncommon friendship will have an uncommon adversary.

Every garden has a snake.

Remember the Garden of Eden. Adam and Eve walked with God in a perfect environment. Yet...the Snake emerged.

Every gift from God will be contested. Severely.

That's why this book is so very important.

Your success depends on your relationships. Completely.

The Bible is The Master Handbook on Relationships; discerning The Master Keys to unlocking the Divine potential in them.

Few have studied relationships more than Dr. Robb Thompson.

Few have ever invested more in their friendships than Dr. Robb Thompson.

Our long years of treasured friendship have enriched my life, unlocked my understanding, and multiplied my celebration of his life. His unique and distinctive ministry reveals an unparalleled life of excellence. His unwavering obsession for excellence has birthed a worldwide audience of protégés who view his mentorship as invaluable, priceless, and essential to their success.

The Ten Critical Laws of Relationship could change your life forever.

Dr. Mike Murdock
Founder and Senior Pastor
The Wisdom Center, Fortworth, Texas

Introduction

We live in a society of extreme commotion and agitation. Lifetimes begin and end in a whirlwind of superficial activity and endless hustling to simply "make a living." Yet, at the core of every person is a desire to discover something deeper. The heart of man possesses profound longings for meaning and purpose. When we make the time to quiet ourselves and do an inward assessment, the questions begin to emerge—Why am I here? Is there a purpose for my life? Is there a specific assignment that I am supposed to fulfill? How do I discover this assignment? And once I do know, how can I ever make it come to pass?

Do you find these questions stirring within you? Are you searching for the insights and tools needed to step into your destiny? If so, you have picked up the right book, because I have discovered a secret that will revolutionize your life. Here it is: ***Those closest to you will determine the outcome of your life.*** In other words, the single most important factor defining your future is *the relationships you embrace.*

Your life is built by relationships. You will receive both the consequences and the rewards of those who are closest to you. Relationships are like buttons on an elevator. Some will take you up, but most will take you down. Some take you up fast, and others take you down fast. Whether you recognize it or not, every relationship you have is taking you somewhere. In fact, these relationships have made you the person you are today, both the good things that you are and every ugly thing that you dislike about yourself.

We live in a very individualistic society, where people take great pride in their independence and ability to stay detached from others. Ever since childhood, they've always wanted to "do it themselves" and prove to the world that they can make it on their own. Invested relationships are seen as unnecessary baggage, a detriment and a hindrance to forward progress. But nothing could be further from the truth. This mentality of independence is dangerous and will lead you down a path of destruction. The wise king Solomon once said, "*A man who isolates himself seeks his own desire; He rages against all wise judgment.*" (Proverbs 18:1) To isolate yourself is to celebrate selfishness. And to celebrate selfishness is to eliminate God from the equation of your life.

Isolation provides a false sense of security. It creates an atmosphere of relational *irresponsibility*. I will discuss this in greater detail as we journey though this book.

Humanity was never built for independence, but rather, for *interdependence*. We begin to realize our highest potential only when we take the risk to believe in one another, become transparent, and celebrate the right people in our lives.

The truths outlined in this book will enable you to maximize every relationship in your life. You will begin to recognize the special relationships that have strategically entered your life to advance you to a higher level of personal effectiveness. You will see that these individuals were sent by God, as Divine links to your future. They are the doorways to your life's purpose!

Once you recognize the fact that God has positioned these people around you to *assist you,* you will no longer feel driven to compete with people. You won't have to try to beat them out of anything, because you will recognize that they have been placed in your life for your improvement, not for your judgment.

These Ten Critical Laws govern every relationship. Understanding them will help you discern the correct posture in any relationship. You will know if you are the teacher or a student, a peer or a protégé, an engine or a caboose. Should you approach the relationship asking questions, or are you expected to make statements and answer questions? Is this a relationship that you must *pursue* for the betterment of your future, or is this a relationship that you must *avoid because of the potential pain that it will create?* This book will answer these and many more of your questions concerning this very critical area of life, relationships.

After twenty years of observing human behavior, I have seen these laws at work in my personal relationships and in those of others that I have been privileged to lead and counsel. Implementing them will unlock the door to your future, your assignment, and your purpose.

Dr. Robb D. Thompson

THE LAW OF
AGREEMENT

IT IS IMPOSSIBLE
TO WALK THRU LIFE WITH ANOTHER,
UNLESS THE CELEBRATION
OF COMMON VALUES IS PRESENT.

1

IT IS IMPOSSIBLE
TO WALK THRU LIFE WITH ANOTHER,
UNLESS THE CELEBRATION OF COMMON VALUES
IS PRESENT.

This first law governs the basic reason why people get into relationship. They must first agree upon a central premise from which they can begin to relate.

Before we get deeper into this law, we must establish a fundamental truism. There is no such thing as an accidental or neutral relationship. Every person you are connected to lives on one side of your relational ledger or the other. They either benefit or hinder your life. Every individual in your life is of consequence to you. They influence you in some way or another, whether you realize it or not. You are continually being seasoned and flavored by the individuals that surround your life. You will actually become like those with whom you associate.

You cannot avoid the influence another brings into your life. Understanding this will cause two things to happen: First, you will begin to seriously examine

> YOU WILL BECOME LIKE THOSE WITH WHOM YOU ASSOCIATE.

each relationship you have, and secondly, you will become very selective in developing new ones. Understanding the power of influence will help you realize the importance of *agreement* concerning foundational issues such as values, beliefs, and ethical standards.

Amos once asked, *"Can two walk together unless they are agreed?"*[1] In other words, before you decide to embrace a relationship with someone, ask yourself this one question: Can I walk in agreement with this individual?

Agreement doesn't mean that you both like to do the same things. It doesn't mean you enjoy the same hobbies or the same movies. It doesn't even mean that you are similar in personality, interests, tastes, family, or work situations.

Agreement means that you both relate on a common ground of inner values. You should want to know what type of values people live by, before you ever start walking in relationship with them. Are they honest? Do they walk in integrity, or are they willing to compromise their standards? Determining the kind of character a person has is crucial to the future success of any relationship.

Examining another man's character is not wrong. In order to ensure that future relationships will benefit your life, you must be willing to examine others. Many of you reading this may find it difficult to do so, because you think, "Who am I, that I

> THE QUALITY OF YOUR LIFE IS GREATLY DEPENDENT UPON THOSE YOU CALL "FRIEND."

can examine another?" I understand where you are coming from. But I have realized that the quality of my life is greatly dependent upon those I call "friend."

Low self-esteem has plagued so many of us. Because of poor self-image, we have befriended people who have either exploited us or, at best, just used us. We find it hard to believe that anyone of good standing would want to be in relationship with us. This self-devaluation is probably the single greatest cause of poor relationships.

1. Amos 3:3

Having relational requirements and criteria doesn't make you better than others; it simply proves that you know your true value. Ask yourself: do I want to become like those I spend time with? Or am I in relationship simply because an individual accepted me as I am?

The right relationships don't just come to us; we have to pursue them. That is the difference between one *falling* into relationship, and another choosing to *step* into relationship with others. But how can you do this? How can you recognize if a person is one with whom you can walk in agreement on the important issues of life?

IDENTIFYING RELATIONSHIPS

Begin by taking a close look at their life. Watch them and observe how they respond in different situations. Ask their family, and even look at their friends. Take a look at their track record. Have they been faithful in the past, or is commitment not one of their strong points? I believe these are some basic ways of identifying the right relationships. But God has given us a clear description of the relationships we ought to embrace. Approximately ten times Solomon tells us, "Do not associate with so and so…"

There are individuals that do not belong in your life. Jesus warned his followers, *"Among you there are sheep in wolves' clothing."*[2] We have embraced these individuals as our friends, and they have hurt us time and time again.

Everyone that comes into your life should not automatically qualify to be your friend. Stick to your principles. As you walk according to a higher standard, you will attract those who do the same. If you ignore the Divine guidelines and choose to build relationships with wrong people, you will put yourself on a dead end street. When choosing relationships, choose people who are pursuing change, growth, and excellence.

---

2. Matthew 7:15, author's paraphrase

I have identified six attributes that must be agreed upon by anyone intending to build positive, progressive relationships. I call them the six non-negotiables of relationship.

THE NON-NEGOTIABLES OF RELATIONSHIP

1. Personal Integrity

The greatest factor determining the outcome of your life is the underlying purpose for which you live. When assessing new relationships, begin by asking yourself, "What is the purpose of his or her life? What drives them to go on? Who are they seeking to please?" These answers will give you insight as to whether you should move forward or hold off, in pursuing the relationship. Search for those who have proven character. *There is no greater attribute than personal integrity.*

Integrity is who a person is. It's the foundation upon which people must build their lives. There is no contractor that would start a project without making sure the foundation met regulation standards. There is no difference when it comes to building our lives and establishing our relationships.

If you are to "walk together" with someone, then you both must be in agreement on this foundational principle—*Our closest allies must always prize integrity above relationship.*

Relationships must serve a greater purpose than simply the enjoyment of mutual interests. When you get with those who are close and dear to your life, the primary purpose is not to relax and have fun. The sole purpose of any relationship is to add value and build a life for one another.

> OUR CLOSEST ALLIES
> MUST ALWAYS
> PRIZE INTEGRITY
> ABOVE RELATIONSHIP.

Solomon said, *"As iron sharpens iron, so a man sharpens the countenance of his friend."*[3] Your commitment to integrity and

3. Proverbs 27:17

Divine principles must always take prece-
dence over your mutual comfort or shared
enjoyments.

Adam and Eve are a prime example of
what *not* to do. Adam compromised his
standards to please his wife. He allowed his

> YOU MAY GET
>
> WHAT YOU WANT,
>
> BUT YOU WILL LOSE
>
> WHAT YOU HAVE.

commitment with Eve to overshadow his commitment to do what was right. In
the end, this compromise destroyed the very thing they were both attempting to
preserve—true intimacy with God and with each other. Remember, *you may get
the short-term gratification that you want, but you will lose the treasure that you
already have.*

Adam pleased Eve, but he lost the garden. David compromised his integrity
for a few moments of pleasure with Bathsheba. Although David ultimately got
Bathsheba, he lost his kingdom. Sampson is another example of compromise. He
compromised his relationship with God for a woman. He got Delilah, but he ultimately lost his life. The list goes on and on. Whatever you compromise to keep,
you will ultimately lose.

Jesus refused to compromise his standards. He pleased God in everything He
did and, as a result, was exalted to the right hand of God. But don't think for a
moment that if Jesus had compromised his standards, that he would have been
exalted. As the old saying goes, "You cannot have both sides of the bread buttered."
Decide today that you will govern your life according to Divine principles and
require integrity from those with whom you relate. You cannot afford to get
involved with the wrong people. Who are these wrong individuals? They are the
ones who want from you what they are not willing to give.

Always be cautious of someone who wants from *you* what he himself is
unwilling to give. For instance, an individual may want loyalty out of you, but he
gives you disloyalty. He wants you to be truthful, but he continues to be dishon-
est. He wants you to love him, but all he gives you is apathy and indifference.
Unfortunately, this is how many good, decent people are destroyed. They tie

> ALWAYS BE CAUTIOUS
>
> OF SOMEONE
>
> WHO WANTS FROM YOU
>
> WHAT HE HIMSELF
>
> IS UNWILLING TO GIVE.

themselves to *users*, who take advantage of an honest person's commitment to integrity, but have no intention of walking in integrity themselves.

Consider this: "*...bad company corrupts good character.*"[4] Seemingly, bad tends to have influence over good, not the other way around. Take Judas, for example. He walked with Jesus for three years, yet he never changed. It is naive to think that we can change people without changing their foundations. My determined purpose has always been to build the foundation of my life on Godly principles. My principles don't change just because the situations or the relationships in my life have been altered. No matter what, I refuse to compromise the principles and values I have already established as a compass for my relational life.

> TO WALK THROUGH
>
> LIFE ACCORDING
>
> TO PRINCIPLE
>
> OFTEN MEANS
>
> YOU MUST WALK ALONE.

Not everyone is interested in taking the proverbial "straight and narrow." To walk through life according to principle often means you must walk alone. But integrity requires you to walk in truth, thus affirming your faithfulness to God and to those with whom you associate.

Integrity also means that as you build relationship, both parties must be willing to speak the truth in love, at the expense of offending each other. Solomon gives us some insight, "*Faithful are the wounds of a friend, but the kisses of an enemy are deceitful.*"[5] Because human beings have a desire to be valued and affirmed, we tend to gravitate towards those who will tell us what we want to hear. We subconsciously surround ourselves with individuals who put on a facade of commitment, because quite frankly, it feels good. But in my observations, this only leads to one place—a place of loneliness, with no bankable relationships to lean on.

---

4. 1 Corinthians 15:33, *NIV*
5. Proverbs 27:6

Refuse to allow anyone into the intimacies of your life, if he or she is unwilling to agree and comply with the proven principles of truth and integrity. A true friend always prizes integrity above relationship. Walk by Divine principle, and soon you will be walking with the right people.

2. A Giving Attitude

One of the greatest types of individuals you can look for are *those who live to give.* Givers are contagious. When you get around a generous individual, all you want to do is give. You have heard it said, "*...It is more blessed to give than to receive.*"[6] The reason this is true is that when you receive something, your harvest is already there; you've gotten your reward, and that's the end of it. However, when you sow, the potential within that seed is a bountiful harvest.

The tendency towards selfishness exists in the heart of every man. There is a voice incessantly droning in our ears, "Your life is too busy for you to try to dispense into somebody else's. You can't even handle what's on your own plate. You need to pull back in your giving—if you spread yourself too thin, you'll be no good to anyone." Many individuals are so consumed with their own lives that they feel they are unable to give into the life of another.

This propensity towards selfishness is celebrated by the society in which we live. The bookstores are filled with best sellers advocating self-indulgence and self-gratification as being the road to self-fulfillment. Most of these authors encourage you to turn your attention inward, towards yourself, in order to feel nurtured and fulfilled. Very few people will tell you the truth—*the path to real happiness, success, and fulfillment is the path of sowing and giving into the lives of others.*

You must strive to be on the giving end of all your relationships. As you give, God will make sure to take care of your needs. You don't need to worry about how you are going to get by. Instead remind yourself, "I have been assigned to solve problems in this individual's life." How can you make that happen? What problems can you solve? Many of us have trouble solving our own problems, let alone the problems of another! That is exactly the quandary. We have been focused on our own problems, rather than solving the problems of those to whom we are

---

6. Acts 20:35

assigned. The more you focus on solving your own problems, the more you will have to do everything on your own.

However, as you focus on meeting the needs of others, God will do His part to meet yours. He promised to supply seed to the sower.[7] As long as you have seed, then you carry the potential of a harvest. But, in order for potential to become a realization, you must first plant the seed. Whether it is money, lending a hand, or giving others encouragement, that is what you must do. Be a giver because *whatever you make happen for others, God will make happen for you.*[8]

> WHATEVER YOU MAKE HAPPEN FOR OTHERS, GOD WILL MAKE HAPPEN FOR YOU.

However, you must strategically plant your seed by sowing your life into good ground—into others who, like yourself, have chosen the lifestyle of a true giver.

This is important for you to understand. If you neglect to sow your life into good soil, you will be left with nothing when harvest time comes. The Bible says, *"If you are too lazy to plow in the right season, you will have no food at the harvest."*[9] This is the reason that so many seniors retire with no one to take care of them. They never sowed their lives into the right people. Through the years, others came into their lives, benefited from their diligence, and then left them all alone.

Remember, God operates this earth by laws. He doesn't respond to need; He responds in direct correlation to the law of the seed. Where you sow your life today will determine where you will be tomorrow.

You must surround yourself with generous people who understand the law of sowing and reaping. Get around those who motivate you to sow. Givers cannot be friends with non-givers. It will be a lopsided relationship that will not last.

You must surround yourself with generous people who understand and practice the grace of giving. If you are a giver, you will not be happy being in relationship with non-givers, because giving isn't just something you *do*—it's *who you are.* And "two cannot walk together unless they agree" on this crucial issue!

---

7. See 2 Corinthians 9: 10
8. Mike Murdock, *My Personal Dream Book* (Denton, TX: The Wisdom Center, 2001), p. 22.
9. Proverbs 20:4

3. Unwavering Commitment to Truth

Truth must be the immovable bedrock of every relationship. In order to function in the realm of certainty, truth must be embraced as *the cornerstone*. All specifications for construction are measured against the unerring, immovable accuracy of the cornerstone of a structure's foundation. If it remains intact, the building will stand strong for many years. However, when this cornerstone is damaged, disregarded, compromised, or removed, the structure will crumble.

Jesus said, *"...You shall know the truth and the truth shall make you free."*[10] The level of commitment to truth determines the level of intimacy that two can enjoy in any relationship. When both parties embrace Truth, they are free to fulfill their destinies. They'll go beyond the mundane, shallow relationships that many endure, to a relationship full of trust and intimacy.

Truth is an integral aspect of every beneficial relationship. You cannot help a person who ignores truth and is continually controlled by his circumstances—nor should you be in relationship with such a person. You cannot help anyone who is unwilling to accept or embrace Divine principle, the greatest source of truth.

> THE LEVEL OF COMMITMENT TO TRUTH DETERMINES THE LEVEL OF INTIMACY THAT TWO CAN ENJOY IN ANY RELATIONSHIP.

Subsequently, you certainly cannot afford to build an intimate relationship with that type of individual.

I practice this principle in my own relationships. I make sure there is an agreement upon a standard of truth that exceeds our individual thoughts and opinions. An objective and indisputable source of truth must be the adjudicator of every aspect of our relationship. It must be made known that when challenges, disagreements, or questions arise, we will always bow our knee in subjection to Divine truth.

When we see *ourselves* as being the source of truth, we have unwittingly placed ourselves simultaneously upon the throne to rule and upon the bench to judge, thus making ourselves the chief cornerstone.

---

10. John 8:32

You have to realize that your *associations* will determine your *assimilations.*
There are some individuals that I enjoy as people. I like their personalities, but I
can't be in relationship with them, because
they disregard truth and do not add value
to my life. Jesus told Peter, *"Get away from
me, Satan! You are a dangerous trap to me.
You are seeing things merely from a human
point of view, and not from God's."*[11] How would you like to be addressed like that?
Would you ever address a close friend in this manner? Jesus did! He clearly prized
integrity and truth above His relationship with Peter. He cared more about pleasing God than offending Peter. Prizing truth above relationship will preserve every
aspect of your life.

> YOUR *ASSOCIATIONS*
> WILL DETERMINE
> YOUR *ASSIMILATIONS.*

4. Long-term Perspective

Although the binding force of past-shared experiences can greatly strengthen
any relationship, you need to focus your attention and energy on *today's pursuits.*
As you run the race God has set before you, it is futile to gaze lingeringly into the
rear-view mirror of your life!

The apostle Paul, in his communication to the church of Philippi, expressed
this same urgency to forget the past and press forward to take hold of the future:

> Friends, don't get me wrong: By no means do I count myself an expert
> in all of this, but I've got my eye on the goal, where God is beckoning us
> onward...I'm off and running, and I'm not turning back.
>
> So let's keep focused on that goal, those of us who want everything God
> has for us. If any of you have something else in mind, something less than
> total commitment, God will clear your blurred vision—you'll see it yet!
> Now that we're on the right track, let's stay on it.
>
> Stick with me, friends. Keep track of those you see running this same
> course, headed for this same goal. There are many out there taking other
> paths, choosing other goals, and trying to get you to go along with them.
> I've warned you of them many times; sadly I'm having to do it again.
> All they want is easy street. They hate Christ's Cross. But easy street is a

---

11. Matthew 16:23, *NLT*

dead-end street. Those who live there make their bellies their gods; belches are their praise; all they can think of is their appetites. But there's far more to life for us.[12]

David said it like this, *"Blessed is the man who walks not in the counsel of the ungodly. Nor stands in the path of sinners, nor sits in the seat of the scornful. But his delight is in the Law of the Lord and in His law he meditates day and night."*[13]

People who are focused on the past will quickly become a weight that will hold you back. You must break free from those relationships and embrace those who will take you to your future. Link yourself up with those who are going somewhere. Seek out those who have a vision for their lives, and find your place at their table. These are the people who will open the door to your destiny. These types of individuals will not waste time, nor are they looking for any short-term fishing buddies!

In October 1975, my life was transformed when I dedicated myself to God. That day, I became a brand new person. I was given a fresh start, with a whole new set of standards. I had a new course set before me and a new purpose for living. To this very day, I have not veered from that course, nor do I ever intend to. Consequently, I

> EVERY RELATIONSHIP YOU HAVE IS EITHER DRAWING YOU CLOSER TO OR FURTHER FROM GOD'S PERFECT WILL FOR YOUR LIFE.

surround myself with those who support that objective. As a new creature, I make sure that *I never make the pleasurable people of my present pay for the painful people of my past.*

Every relationship you have is either drawing you closer to or further from God's perfect will for you life. Every person who surrounds you should be pushing you to reach your objective. Jesus had an objective, *"...I do not seek My own will but the will of the Father who sent Me."*[14] Jesus was more concerned about pleasing God than offending man. As He brought help and direction to the lives of others, Jesus surrounded Himself with those who were there to help Him fulfill God's will for His life. He did not seek shallow or short-term relationships. When He said,

12. Philippians 3:12-20, Eugene Peterson, *The Message New Testament With Psalms and Proverbs* (Colorado Springs, CO: NavPress Publishing Group, 1993, 1994, 1995), p. 493-494.
13. Psalm 1:1-2
14. John 5:30

"Follow Me" He actually implied, "Follow me for the rest of your life."

Jesus had purpose behind everything He did, especially when it came to rela-

tionships. He was in it for the long haul.
He was in relationship to add value and to
help others fulfill the God-given purpose
for their lives. He cared about nothing else.
Even the Pharisees made the statement,
"…*Teacher, we know that You are true and*
care about no one; for You do not regard the
person of men, but teach the way of God in truth…"[15]

> I NEVER MAKE THE
> PLEASURABLE PEOPLE
> OF MY PRESENT PAY FOR
> THE PAINFUL PEOPLE
> OF MY PAST.

Although Jesus cared about people, He cared *more* about pleasing God. As followers of righteousness, we also must become serious about fulfilling God's plan and purpose for our lives. If anyone becomes a liability and drags you back into your past, you must be willing to let go of that relationship; and letting go is quite painful.

Before you step into a relationship, know that you can commit for the long haul. If you cannot commit, then don't say you can. David commended the person "…*who swears to his own hurt and does not change.*"[16] The inability to see long-term is the cause for the present divorce rate. Couples are not willing to be committed to the end. They look at what they can get short-term, and then when something better comes along, they leave. In any type of relationship, a long-term perspective is a necessary attribute. It will cause two individuals to overlook present trouble and move toward greener pastures.

5. The Passionate Pursuit of Distinction

We must seek to get around individuals who challenge us to grow. Don't allow yourself to be satisfied with a mediocre or ordinary way of living. A casual attitude towards life will only lead you to a place of disappointment and defeat. If you want to realize the best for your life, then you must launch out on a lifelong pursuit of excellence.

People often say they want excellence in their lives, but then they stop pursuing it because the cost is too great. They become discouraged and quit when

15. Mark 12:14
16. Psalm 15:4

they realize that excellence requires a daily striving for improvement. They aren't willing to pay the price to obtain the prize. Excellence is something you have to go after all the time. Surround yourself with others who are sold out to the quest of making their best even better. These are the types of individuals who will take you to a greater tomorrow.

But, what does it mean to be excellent? Most people can only tell you their opinion of excellence. They don't understand how powerful the concept really is. Let me give you an idea of all that is encompassed in the word excellence.

Excellence is meritoriously near the standard, or the model, by which we are all measured. It is imminently good, the best of its kind. It is a virtue, a state of being—a part of who a person is, not just what a person does. Excellence **can** be obtained, because it is measurable. You can see excellence in the life of a person who is always moving toward improvement. He's always getting better.

If you don't go after what you want, it is safe to say you really don't want it. So many people say they want to be excellent, yet they don't pursue it, nor do they pursue those who are excellent. Instead, they live their lives in mediocrity, with a "just good enough" attitude. Year after year, they stay right in the middle of the pack, not craving excellence enough to trade their time for it.

Stay away from the mediocre individual who is satisfied with where he or she is. Mediocrity is an infectious and contagious disease, one that will penetrate deep into the crevices of your life and squelch any desire for personal improvement. Mediocre people will halt any progress you have made. They disguise themselves by saying the right things, but ultimately they are in your life to hinder your future progress.

Remember when Heaven is ready to multiply you, Hell assigns people to put an end to you. That is why having non-negotiable criteria for relationship is so important. You must recognize those individuals whom God has brought into your life—those who are the people of your tomorrow. Failure to recognize them can potentially destroy your life.

6. A Kingdom Mentality

Here is a driving principle: <u>The kind of requirements you place upon others</u> <u>reveals the kind of person that you are yourself.</u> Read it again. Memorize it and live it. Your actions will quickly uncover who you really are. You cannot separate who you are from what you do. Many Christians have attempted to do this. They claim to be Christians, yet they live like unbelievers. In relationship, it is important that you *watch what a person does and stop just listening to what a person says.*

> THE KIND OF REQUIREMENTS YOU PLACE UPON OTHERS REVEALS THE KIND OF PERSON THAT YOU ARE YOURSELF.

James tells us, *"But someone will say, 'You have faith, and I have works.' Show me your faith without your works, and I will show you my faith by my works."*[17] You must believe only what another does, not what he says. You must learn to watch a person's feet.

In determining who a person is, just spend some time with him and you will soon discover what he truly believes. Ask questions of his friends, family, and especially his spiritual leaders, concerning his character and attitudes. Don't just allow anyone into your life. If someone truly wants to be your friend, they must be willing to undergo this essential examination.

> WATCH WHAT A PERSON DOES AND STOP JUST LISTENING TO WHAT A PERSON SAYS.

Once again, if you ignore these fundamental differences, you will end up destroying your life. Think about this: *"He who walks with wise men will be wise, but the companion of fools will be destroyed."*[18] Wrong people will damage your life. Right people will multiply your life.

When you link yourself with those who see life from an eternal perspective, you elevate your relationships to a level that is not easily hampered by temporal setbacks. Take some time and ask yourself, "Where are my relationships taking me?" *Every* relationship is taking you somewhere. Identifying the direction you

---

17. James 2:18
18. Proverbs 13:20

are headed is a key determinant of whether or not to continue the relationship.

Obedience to Godly principle is a magnet that will draw the right people into your life. By walking in obedience everyday, you'll attract others who are willing to make the sacrifices and changes that are necessary to help you reach your full potential. Your true potential is not independent of others. You are designed for interdependence, and therefore, you will go only as far as those with whom you associate on a daily basis. Only by pursuing Divinely ordained relationships and remaining faithful to the end will you maximize your potential, and thus fulfill the destiny to which you've been called.

Jesus revealed a criterion He had for friendship, when he said, *"You are my friends if you do whatever I command you."*[19] The willingness to obey Divine precepts is an attribute that you must seek in every relationship. Your obedience coupled with the obedience of another will propel that relationship to higher heights.

Obedience became the pivotal factor for a young man named Elisha. Day after day, year after year, he dutifully served his mentor, Elijah. He pursued Elijah knowing that *he could only possess what he was willing to pursue.*[20]

The day finally came when that pursuit paid off:

> When they came to the other side [of the Jordan River], Elijah said unto Elisha, "What can I do for you, before I am taken away?"
>
> And Elisha replied, "Please, let me become your rightful successor [let a double portion of your spirit be upon me]."
>
> "You have asked a difficult thing," Elijah replied. "If you see me when I am taken away from you, then you will get your request; but if not, then you won't."[21]

Elisha did, in fact, receive the mantle that he had so diligently pursued. But what was the key that unlocked such power and favor in his life? Elijah told Elisha, "If you see *me* when I'm gone, the inheritance on my life will be yours. But if you don't see me when I'm gone, you will inherit nothing."

Longevity of commitment is the key. *I will experience my greatest moments and fulfill the destiny to which I've been called only as I remain faithful to Divinely*

19. John 15:14
20. Mike Murdock, *The Leadership Secrets of Jesus* (Dallas, TX: Honor Books, 1996), p. 24.
21. 2 Kings 2:9-10, *NLT*

> I WILL EXPERIENCE MY GREATEST MOMENTS AND FULFILL THE DESTINY TO WHICH I'VE BEEN CALLED ONLY AS I REMAIN FAITHFUL TO DIVINELY ORDAINED RELATIONSHIPS.

ordained relationships. This revelation has revolutionized my relationships. It has caused me to turn up the intensity level of my pursuit, because it is my desire to carry on the legacy of my patriarchs when they are gone. I want my spiritual fathers to know *today,* that I have avowed with them in united purpose. When they have finished their portion of this race, I *will* be the faithful son that carries the torch of their legacy into the future. For, it is not the protégé's words or intentions that will secure him an inheritance. It is the protégé's *longevity of commitment* that will deliver to him the double portion.

Let's recap. These are the six non-negotiable attributes of any fulfilling relationship:

1. Personal Integrity

2. A Giving Attitude

3. An Unswerving Commitment to Truth

4. A Long-Term Perspective and Commitment

5. A Passionate Pursuit of Distinction

6. A Kingdom Mentality

These are the governing characteristics of every successful relationship. Lacking any one of these will constitute a crack in the foundation of our relationships. Refuse to walk intimately with anyone who does not possess the six attributes listed above. If you cannot find anyone around you, patiently cultivate these traits within yourself, and soon you will attract the right people into your life.

THE LAW OF AGREEMENT

It is impossible to walk thru life with another,
unless the celebration of common values is present.

+ You will become like those with whom you associate.

+ The quality of your life is greatly dependent upon those you call "friend."

+ Our closest allies must always prize integrity above relationship.

+ You may get what you want, but you will lose what you have.

+ Always be cautious of someone who wants from you what he himself is unwilling to give.

+ To walk through life according to principle often means you must walk alone.

+ Whatever you make happen for others, God will make happen for you.

+ The level of commitment to truth determines the level of intimacy that two can enjoy in any relationship.

+ Your *associations* will determine your *assimilations.*

+ Every relationship you have is either drawing you closer to or further from God's perfect will for your life.

+ I never make the pleasurable people of my present pay for the painful people of my past.

+ The kind of requirements you place upon others reveals the kind of person that you are yourself.

+ Watch what a person does and stop just listening to what a person says.

+ I will experience my greatest moments and fulfill the destiny to which I've been called *only* as I remain faithful to Divinely ordained relationships.

THE LAW OF
ACCESS

THERE ARE UNSPOKEN RULES
BOTH TO ACCESS AND TO REMAIN IN RELATIONSHIP.

2

THERE ARE UNSPOKEN RULES
BOTH TO ACCESS AND TO REMAIN
IN RELATIONSHIP.

Every relationship has rules both to enter and to remain. The practice of *qualifying* relationships is a rare one among people today. Many have bought into the lie that we should welcome everyone that comes into our lives. We must realize that every relationship has either a positive or a negative effect on our life. If that effect is not a positive one, then even through tears we must be willing to turn away from that relationship.

For years, both men and women have disregarded the practice of qualification. They argue that one is arrogant to say others must qualify to be in relationship with him or her. Many have asked me, "Who do you think you are, making others qualify for relationship with you?" Honestly, I understand who I'm not, but I also know who I am. I am a child of God, and I understand there is an enemy that is attempting to destroy my life. He can only get to me by using others. That is the very reason Solomon said many times, *do not associate with this or that type of individual.*

The Scriptures clearly show us that even Jesus was cautious about committing Himself to people. (Remember, He knew all men.)[1] He knew the true man hidden behind the religious mask. He saw into their hearts. He was careful to guard his heart because of what Solomon stated, *"Keep your heart with all diligence, for out of it spring the issues of life."*[2]

A broken heart is simply the fruit of an unscrupulous relationship. I have seen it too many times; individuals of all ages sitting across the table from me, talking about the pain of the relationships they have been in. For years, I didn't understand this—why would people pursue pain? Why would they pursue a relationship that was going to hurt them? I now understand why individuals make such a destructive decision.

> A BROKEN HEART IS THE FRUIT OF AN UNSCRUPULOUS RELATIONSHIP.

We all have a desire within us to be accepted. Nobody likes to be rejected. Hence, we have accepted the wrong people into our lives and have entered certain relationships simply because they are willing to accept us as we are. This fear of rejection has been the author of countless damaging relationships. Negative people have accessed our lives, only to hurt us in the end.

If you want to have a successful and purposeful life, you must continually fight the constant pressure of negative people coming into your life. The only way one can maintain a stable life is through pursuing and maintaining right relationships. You cannot afford to get involved with the wrong types of people. You must understand that *you will suffer both the consequences and the rewards of those who are closest to you.*

> YOU WILL SUFFER BOTH THE CONSEQUENCES AND THE REWARDS OF THOSE WHO ARE CLOSEST TO YOU.

As we saw earlier, Solomon warned, *"He who walks with wise men will be wise, but the companion of fools will be*

1. See John 2:24
2. Proverbs 4:23

destroyed."³ That word *destroyed* does not necessarily mean dead or absent from life, but it is talking about the *death of one's purpose.* The moment you or I move toward the direction of a wrong relationship is the moment that our purpose begins to fade away. It is vital that you qualify every person that comes into your life.

TYPES OF RELATIONSHIP

At this very moment there are three types of individuals in your life:

1. *Yesterday people*—Those from your past, who continually try to drag you into your past.
2. *Today people*—Those who are willing to accept you in the state where they first met you, and have some role to play in helping you fulfill your present assignment.
3. *Future bearers (tomorrow people)*—Those who are undeniably tied to helping you enter your future. They have been where you want to go. They are the only ones who can take you into a better tomorrow. Other terms given to these types of individuals are 'mentor,' 'father,' 'pastor,' and 'teacher.' Very few individuals ever access future bearers, because quite frankly, the qualifications are very high.

Every relationship is moving you either towards or away from the fulfillment of God's purpose for your life. You must choose each relationship wisely and refuse to compromise the set of standards that govern your life. These standards will determine the types of individuals you attract. You must establish Divine principles to govern your every action, and posture as one who is unwilling to compromise your values for a relationship. This commitment to principle will greatly alter the quality of your relationships.

Principle-centered living also qualifies you for relationship with those further along than you. But as you begin to move toward the relationships that will take you into your future, you must first understand the protocol that governs those

---

3. Proverbs 13:20

relationships. You will need to posture differently in every relationship. Knowing who you are and what posture to take is a critical element in relational success.

Future bearers and tomorrow people are necessary if you are ever going to fulfill God's will for your life. These are the individuals you must sit under and learn from. But only when you understand how to posture under them will you enter into relationship with them. My main focus throughout this chapter is to show you how to accurately *access* the future bearers that enter your life.

PROTOCOL

Protocol is a vital ingredient to the success of any relationship. Protocol is a term given to the rules that govern how to enter and how to remain in any relationship.

> PROTOCOL
>
> IS A TERM GIVEN TO
>
> THE RULES THAT GOVERN
>
> HOW TO ENTER AND
>
> HOW TO REMAIN
>
> IN ANY RELATIONSHIP.

As I have already mentioned, every environment and every relationship has unspoken rules for entering and for remaining. Whenever I go to a foreign country, I am briefed on the protocol of that particular country. In certain countries, you cannot walk behind a dignitary. You have to walk in front of him. In other countries, it is a blatant sign of disrespect if you walk in front of a dignitary. If you have achieved greatness in his sight, *maybe* you can walk alongside him, but you never walk in front of him.

Protocol protects you from ever taking a relationship for granted. In order to ensure this right code of behavior, you must regularly examine every relationship that you are in. Be careful not to take presumptive steps in a relationship. And never *assume* that access has been granted to you. Wait for an invitation. Once you've been invited, passionately pursue that individual. But don't allow yourself to take God-ordained relationships for granted.

Never allow the invitation of intimacy to be destroyed by the contempt of familiarity. In other words, never take a relationship for granted, because in doing so, you allow a very important relationship to become too familiar. This happens when you stop esteeming your relationships as valuable, and you become somewhat casual in the way you relate to that person. As soon as you develop an intimate relationship with an individual, you must work at maintaining the same level of respect that you had expressed at the beginning. Never let the invitation to intimacy bring you to a place where you no longer hold that person in high esteem.

> NEVER ALLOW THE INVITATION OF INTIMACY TO BE DESTROYED BY THE CONTEMPT OF FAMILIARITY.

Always treat the relationships God gives you with high admiration. Determine that you will never let go of them. This is especially true when relating to authority. The writer of Proverbs tells us, *"...And he who waters will also be watered himself."*[4] Become a refreshing spring to those around you. Seek to be a blessing to them every time you step into their presence.

All successful people understand protocol. A few Biblical examples include Joseph, Ruth, and Esther. When Joseph was summoned by Pharaoh, he chose to shave, take a bath, and change his clothes before entering the Pharaoh's presence. At that time, the Israelites customarily did not shave, but instead, wore beards. However, Joseph chose to show respect for the Pharaoh by complying with the Egyptian protocol of being clean-shaven.

When Ruth was scheduled to meet Boaz, she was instructed by Naomi, her mother-in-law, to wash and anoint herself with her best perfume, and wear her best clothes. Naomi also gave Ruth specific instructions concerning the proper way to approach Boaz. She understood that timing and posture were extremely important when seeking favor from an esteemed individual.

---

4. Proverbs 11:25

In preparation for her time to be with King Ahasuerus, Esther bathed in perfumed oil for twelve months, as was standard practice. Following her year of bathing, Esther went to the king's eunuch to ask advice concerning how best to approach the king. When all of the rest of the maidens were going to other women to ask how to please the king, wise Esther went to the king's eunuch and said: "What does the king like? What does he want? How do I please him? What protocol does the king embrace? How do I enter his presence? How do I remain? How do I act while I'm there? How do I bow before him? *How do I please him?*"

Knowing the right protocol will open doors for you. It will take you further than your personality or talent ever could. To be successful in building valuable relationships, you must be mindful of the underlying codes of behavior—the rules that gain you entrance into an individual's life. And keep in mind that although posturing correctly will grant you access, only by becoming what another needs, will you remain.

DISCERNING THE CORRECT POSTURE

I have discovered that one of the most important aspects in the arena of relationship is the way that I posture myself with others. All meaningful interaction ceases the moment I violate posturing protocol.

In every relationship, there is proper way to posture. This positioning will be different in every association that you have. To posture correctly, you must know who you are called to be, in any given relationship. If you are postured incorrectly, you and those around you will not gain any benefit from the relationship.

For example, in one relationship you may be expected to position yourself as a student, but in another relationship, as a teacher. Throughout any given day, I personally have to posture as a husband, a pastor, a teacher, a counselor, a father, a spiritual father, a boss, a businessman, and a friend. It is very important to me that I put myself in the correct position, in any given relationship. I never assume a role that has not been granted to me. I humbly embrace the position given to me, and I choose to be happy with whatever that may be. Only when I have properly postured myself am I able to truly give or receive in relationship.

> ONLY WHEN I HAVE PROPERLY POSTURED MYSELF AM I ABLE TO TRULY GIVE OR RECEIVE IN RELATIONSHIP.

I have the privilege of knowing some great men and women around the world, but I don't try to be a spiritual mentor to them. Should they discover something in me that they like, that is fine. But until that day, I posture myself according to my relationship with each of them—a servant willing to become whatever they need.

Even if a person is my peer and equal, I choose to assume the role of a servant. Rather than serving them in the same way I serve those above me, I serve them with my love, support, encouragement, openness, and fellowship.

Then, there are those whom God has placed under my authority. I am called to speak into their lives. I am not there to be their friend, but to teach them, train them, and lead them.

You, too, have a position in each relationship you have with others. Remember, the purpose of relationship is to add value to one another. This can only be accomplished when you have examined yourself and have taken the role you are called to play in each of your relationships.

Take some time and examine your relationships in light of the following questions:

+ Who initiated this relationship?
+ For what purpose was it established?
+ What is expected of me in this relationship?
+ What am I being asked to do?
+ Am I pursuing access and favor from someone, or am I being asked to grant access and favor to someone?
+ Am I a son, a father, or a brother/sister/peer in this relationship?

+ What is it I hope to impart into this relationship?
+ What is it I hope to obtain from this relationship?
+ What need is being met by this relationship that no other relationship can meet?
+ Would I consider this a necessary relationship in my life, or an optional one?
+ What would my future look like without this person in my life?
+ Would the other person consider my presence necessary or optional?
+ How can I best please the other person in this relationship?
+ How can I best please God in this relationship?

Answering these questions will help you to discern your proper role in every relationship. Posture yourself correctly, and you will set the stage for future success in all that you do.

WHY ACCESS IS GRANTED

In Chapter One we discussed the types of individuals you should look to associate with; but how can we enter into relationship with mentors and fathers, those who far exceed us, both in achievements and wisdom? What are the requirements to access a mentor or father? What qualities must you possess in order to ensure an invitation to sit at the feet of a mentor? I have outlined ten essential qualities that must be cultivated and developed in a person's life before he or she can access the great. Never forget: *Future access will always be granted the moment you choose to bring pleasure to those who are important to your life.*

> FUTURE ACCESS WILL ALWAYS BE GRANTED THE MOMENT YOU CHOOSE TO BRING PLEASURE TO THOSE WHO ARE IMPORTANT TO YOUR LIFE.

These ten qualities will ensure that you become pleasing to those whom you serve. But, before I discuss these qualities, I want to remind you that *every relationship feeds either a strength or a weakness within a person.* Depending on the strength or weakness of an individual's character, he will posture himself in one of two distinct ways, when pursuing a relationship with the great: *he will either be a prodigal or a protégé.* **In order to access the great you must posture as a protégé.**

A prodigal is a person who is in a relationship *only to take.* They are unwilling or unable to contribute life to the relationship, but rather, they are what I like to call 'relational vampires'—they suck the life out of the relationship. In studying how people interact with one another, I have observed that each and every one of us has to be cautious of these so-called "prodigals."

These prodigals display very distinct motives and behaviors, which will be discussed and highlighted throughout this book. It is my hope that you will examine yourself and your relationships in light of this information, and take the necessary steps to rid yourself of any relationship harboring these parasitic tendencies.

> EVERY RELATIONSHIP
> FEEDS A STRENGTH
> OR A WEAKNESS
> WITHIN YOU.

A prodigal is a person who is in a relationship only *to take* whatever is available for the taking. Prodigals do not add value to the relationship, but rather, they leave a bitter aroma of pain and brokenness.

To help you recognize a prodigal, I have outlined some basic attributes and tendencies:

1. **A prodigal wants what you have, but is unwilling to pay the same price to obtain it.**

2. **A prodigal is interested in what you will do for his influence and reputation.**

3. **A prodigal is there solely to get.**

4. **A prodigal wants you to continually recognize and praise him for his achievements, but he is not interested in celebrating yours.**

5. **A prodigal believes you are in his life to meet his needs, but he is not there to meet yours.**

6. **A prodigal is in your life looking for credibility, rather than correction and instruction.**

7. **A prodigal will embrace your enemies, but still want to be your friend.**

8. **A prodigal will use any knowledge to manipulate and use you.**

9. **A prodigal will leave, the moment he has received from you what he believes that he needs.**

10. **A prodigal will get angry with you for attempting to correct him.**

These are just a few tendencies of a prodigal, but I believe this will give you adequate knowledge in order to recognize one that may attempt to come into your life. Remember, they say the right things, but their actions say something else. It has been said, "Your actions speak so loudly that I can't hear a thing you are saying." Listen with your eyes, and watch out for these types of people.

On the contrary, a protégé or a son is looking to sow his life into the one who is called to lead him. Protégés understand that no seed can ever produce a harvest unless it dies and is planted into good ground. Therefore, you must choose to lay your life down in service to the esteemed man or woman to whom you are called.

A true protégé knows he must demonstrate the following ten qualities in order to be granted access to the great:

1. Pursuit

A mentor or father doesn't need to know what you know, regardless of how much you know. Jesus said it like this, *"Most assuredly I say to you, a servant is not greater than his master, nor is he who is sent greater than he who sent him."*[5] These individuals have years of experience. It is your responsibility to pursue their wisdom and serve them with all your heart. *A protégé makes it his aim to pursue his mentor.*

> A PRODIGAL WANTS THE MENTOR TO PURSUE HIM; A PROTÉGÉ MAKES IT HIS AIM TO PURSUE HIS MENTOR.

Find out what it takes to draw wisdom from your mentor, in order to unlock the

5. John 13:16

future God has for you. Although the invitation to access is granted by the mentor, the responsibility to come to the party is on the part of the protégé. A prodigal, however, wants the mentor to pursue him.

Elisha exemplifies this principle so well. Remember, after all the sons of the prophets were long gone, Elisha continued to pursue. Elisha told Elijah, *"As long as you live and as the Lord lives, I will never leave you. I am committed to you until the very end."*[6]

Any opportunity to leave or step out of relationship with those above you will reveal your true heart. A protégé will say, as Elisha said, "As long as you live and as long as the Lord lives, I will never leave you." *The reward of any relationship is determined by the value that is placed upon it.*

> THE REWARD OF ANY RELATIONSHIP IS DETERMINED BY THE VALUE THAT IS PLACED UPON IT.

Your pursuit in relationship should not be to receive a temporary blessing, but an eternal inheritance. You must understand an inheritance is never given until the father is gone. But, if you leave before the inheritance comes, you have lost your claim to it.

Your reward only comes when you don't waver or cease from pursuing your mentor. You must stick close to those you are pursuing. Earnestly seek their wisdom, and diligently follow their counsel. Only when you do will you enjoy the rewards of pursuit. Please don't forget, the responsibility of relationship lies on the one pursuing rather than the one being pursued.

2. Respect

Respect is a magnet. It will instantly draw towards you the object of your respect. Respect will give you entrance to intimacy in the lives of others. It will take you to secret places where only a few are allowed to go.

> RESPECT IS MAGNETIC. IT WILL ATTRACT PEOPLE, WHILE DISRESPECT WILL REPEL THEM.

6. 2 Kings 2:2, author's paraphrase

Showing respect towards others reveals a lot about your character. It reveals that *you* are a person of dignity and self-respect, for you cannot give something that you do not possess. Being a respectful person shows that you place great value on the lives of others, and therefore, you are someone who can be trusted with the valuable secrets of another's heart. Treating others with respect and dignity uncovers a confident and selfless spirit that strives to put others' needs ahead of its own.

> A PRODIGAL RESPECTS
> WITH HIS WORDS,
> BUT NOT WITH HIS HEART;
> A PROTÉGÉ LETS
> HIS ACTIONS BE THE
> SPOKESMAN OF HIS HEART.

Conversely, disrespect will immediately repel others. Doors of access will be closed and locked tight against a disrespectful attitude. A disrespectful person is struggling with his own self-abasement—the disrespect he feels towards himself is what he reflects outward to others. He cannot be trusted with intimacy or wisdom, because he doesn't understand its inestimable value. No one is eager to develop a deeper relationship with a disrespectful person—it is just too costly.

Respect is the key that opens the door of access. It is one of the greatest attributes you can possess. Without it, no marriage can stay strong and no family can stay together. Without respect, no employee can be promoted and no relationship can grow. The Apostle Paul stated, *"Out of respect for Christ, be courteously reverent to one another."* The respect I show towards others is a by-product of my relationship with God. I respect others not because of how they treat me, but because they are created in the image of God. He loves and values them, and

> DON'T RELATE
> TO PEOPLE THROUGH GOD,
> BUT RELATE
> TO GOD THROUGH PEOPLE.

so should I. If they are the objects of His love, then they are certainly worthy of my respect. For this reason, *I don't relate to people through God, but I relate to God through people.*

The disintegration and failure of so

---

7. Ephesians 5:21, *NLT*, author's paraphrase

many relationships can be traced to the neglect of one attribute—Respect. The failure of any marriage is a direct result of the neglect of respect. The breakdown of any relationship between a parent and a child is also linked to the neglect of respect. Respect is required as part of the underlying foundation of all relationships, regardless of the culture you live in.

3. Honor

When you honor someone, you are placing value upon him or her. Honor is making a commitment to always value and respect someone. You must expand your definition of what honor means, by including the *commitment* aspect. For healthy relationships, you must honor everyone. You may not like them based on how you feel about them, but you should still honor—that is, to treat them as though they are valuable, for God has already declared that they are.

> HONOR IS THE GATE THROUGH WHICH ALL GODLY RELATIONSHIPS ENTER.

Without a doubt, the concept of honor is the single most important principle I know of for building healthy relationships. *Honor is the gate through which all Godly relationships enter.*

Honor is not only the foundation of all successful relationships, but it lies at the heart of every successful individual. God tells us, and has told humanity for thousands of years, to honor others. He promised us that if we honor, then we would live a long life full of blessings. I am not sure about you, but I want that in my life!

But, what is honor? The Hebrew word for "honor" is *kabed*. It literally gives us a picture of *heaviness* or *weightiness*. "To honor" is *to give great weight, importance, worth, and significance to something or someone.* On the contrary, the word dishonor gives us a picture of something 'light and trivial'—one of mist or steam.

When you honor people, you are conveying to them that they hold a certain weight in your heart. You are communicating to them that they are valuable to you. When you dishonor someone, you treat the relationship lightly, suggesting to them that they are neither valuable nor significant. This can be done many different ways, but many times it is done through your body language and your attitude.

Dishonor stems from one's heart, and eventually reveals itself in one's actions. Remember, man looks at the outward actions, but God is looking at your heart. Do you honor those above you *from your heart*, or just with your words? Do you value their presence and wisdom? Take some time to think about what you can do to show honor toward them. I guarantee it will make a huge difference in your relationships. And, you will be favored for doing so.

Learn how to honor others, especially those above you. Find out what pleases them, and become what they need for you to become. Being honorable is so important. There is no greater way of honoring a mentor then bowing your knee, for the sole purpose of bringing them pleasure.

4. Attitude

Put simply, relationships just work better when you are happy. A good attitude goes a long way toward building lasting relationships. I mean, nobody wants to be around a person harboring a bad attitude, do they? The fact is that the friendlier you are, the more you are going to have people who want to pursue long-lasting, mutually beneficial relationships with you. Encourage yourself, put on a smile, and speak only kind words to others. Treat people with a great deal of joyfulness, and you will see your relationships greatly improve.

It is easy to understand why so many people go unrewarded in life. They just don't do the necessary things to be rewarded. Although life is designed to be a continual ascension, most people stop ascending. You must be willing to cheerfully solve problems for those God has placed in your life. Only when you begin to solve problems with a positive attitude will you be granted access into a mentor's life. Through the prophet Isaiah, God spoke these words, *"If you are willing and obedient, you shall eat the best from the land."*[8] Notice, he said be *willing* and not just obedient. God wants our willingness, as well as our obedience.

Many individuals just exist, going through life unwilling to serve those around them. Then they wonder why their relationships are dry and shallow. You cannot grumble about life and, at the same time, expect to enjoy the reward of access. A

8. Isaiah 1:19, *NIV*

poor attitude, left unchecked, has been the deathblow to innumerable relationships.

> JOY MUST BE THE ATTITUDE OF CHOICE LONG BEFORE YOU KNOW THE OUTCOME OF YOUR CIRCUMSTANCES.

Attitude plays just as great a role, if not greater, as that of solving problems. Everyone loves an individual with a great attitude. How has your attitude been, as of late? Do those above you know that you *enjoy* following their instruction? Are they persuaded by your positive attitude? *Joy must be your attitude of choice long before you know the outcome of your circumstances!*

Nothing guarantees failure or success like a person's attitude. Attitude is *everything*. Your attitude determines which path you're on, as you move toward your future. An excellent attitude will set you on a path of favor, promotion, and success. A poor attitude will lead you down the path of compromise, loss, and defeat. In a society where the outcome of our lives can, at times, appear to rest so heavily on the decisions of others, this is one area that *only you* can change. No one can *make* you have a poor attitude; and no one can force you to have a good one. When it comes to your attitude, it is entirely up to you!

Access is granted to those who exhibit a consistently great attitude. An excellent attitude will quickly get you noticed by those who can promote you in life. It will open doors of opportunity and favor reserved only for those with grateful, generous dispositions. A wise person under-stands that his *attitude* in life will determine his *altitude* in life. An excellent attitude is the tool God uses to build an extraordinary future for you and your family.

> YOUR ATTITUDE IN LIFE WILL DETERMINE YOUR ALTITUDE IN LIFE.

5. Attention

Knowing how to invest your time and attention will give you access to the great. We must stop *spending time* and start *investing time*. In this rat-race world, time has become a person's most valuable commodity. It is also the element that puts all of us on the same playing field; we are each given twenty-four hours in a day—no more, no less. What we focus on in each twenty-four hour period will determine the outcome of our lives.

> A TRUE SERVANT
> GLADLY ABANDONS
> ALL PERSONAL PLEASURE,
> IN ORDER TO BECOME
> A TOOL IN THE HAND
> OF THE ONE HE SERVES.

People invest time and attention into what they love and what they believe is important. The way that I prove my love and respect for someone is by giving him my full, undivided attention. I prove he is important to me by paying attention to the things he likes, what he enjoys to do, what pleases him, etc. I also pay attention to what angers him, what irritates him, and what breaks his heart, and I choose, on purpose, to be a problem-solver in those arenas. My goal, at all times, is to make his needs and desires more important than my own. *A true servant gladly abandons all personal pleasure, in order to become a tool in the hand of the one he serves.*

Obviously, a person cannot give this kind of focus and attention to *many* relationships. If he tried, he would end up spreading himself too thin in *all* of his relationships, and would experience real benefit from *none* of them. A wise person will focus his seed, sowing *deeply* into the lives of a few, instead of sowing *shallowly* into the lives of many.

A servant is interested in the *details* of another's life. When you pay attention to the smallest of details, you will never fail in the big assignments of life. A protégé looks

> A PRODIGAL
> IS INTERESTED IN THE
> DETAILS OF HIS OWN LIFE;
> A PROTÉGÉ
> IS INTERESTED IN THE
> DETAILS OF ANOTHER'S.

to follow the instructions of his mentor "to a t." He is attentive to every instruction, however small it might be, making sure to do all that is asked of him. We must never allow the ones we are pursuing to be forced to look in another direction for the solution to their problems. That is our ticket. That is our place not someone else's!

We see this quality in the life of Joseph. Joseph understood that *immediate attention to detail gets the immediate attention of the one whom you seek to please.*

When Joseph initially began to work for Potiphar as a slave, he quickly excelled in every area to which he was assigned. That quality got him noticed by Potiphar. His attention to detail made him stand out from the rest of Potiphar's slaves. No matter what Joseph was instructed to do, he did it. Then, after completing the task, he came back and asked, "What else would you have for me to do?"

> IMMEDIATE ATTENTION TO DETAIL GETS THE IMMEDIATE ATTENTION OF THE ONE WHOM YOU SEEK TO PLEASE.

Focus is extremely important in relationship. I find that the more I can focus my attention in relationship, the quicker the doors of opportunity will open. Multiplication of favor, promotion, and blessing always follows a seed of *focused attention.* As I lose my life by pouring attention into the life of another, I discover that I *find* my life.

6. A Gift—Your Seed and Skill

Ponder this for a moment: *"A man's gift makes room for him, and brings him before great men."*[9] Your gifts will open doors for you. But, you also must remember that the only gifts that will ever be remembered will be the gifts that the individual *wanted.*

Each and every person has something particular he or she wants to receive in life. I study and look for what my superiors want. Then, I choose to plant the kind of seed in that person's life that *he* wants to receive, not just the kind *I* want to give him. Thus, I become significant in his life and I am granted further access.

> A PRODIGAL WANTS TO EXPLOIT THE MENTOR'S GIFTS AND SKILLS TO BECOME GREAT; A PROTÉGÉ WANTS TO DEVELOP HIS GIFTS AND SKILLS TO THE END THAT HIS MENTOR WOULD BE GREAT.

---

9. Proverbs 18:16

Not only will a material gift grant you access, but a God-given ability and gifting will also cause your mentor to notice you. It is your gift that just may be the answer to his problem. If you are able to multiply his efforts and add value to his life through your abilities, then access will be granted. So, take an inventory of the gifts that God has placed within you and begin to develop them, knowing that they will make room for you before great men and women.

Also, let me say, that even if you don't have certain gifts that a mentor is looking for, you have the ability to develop new skills. If you can hone specific skills, you will greatly enhance your chance for future access.

7. Obedience

The proof of real love will be evident in a person's actions, not his words. You must always be willing to prove everything you say by backing it up with your actions. Remember, people do not believe what they tell you; people believe *what they do*. *The crown of a man's character and purpose is born the moment he realizes his duty to obey.*

> THE CROWN OF A MAN'S CHARACTER AND PURPOSE IS BORN THE MOMENT HE REALIZES HIS DUTY TO OBEY.

Even actions can sometimes be deceiving. Many people outwardly obey in order to mask inward rebellion. True obedience begins with a tender, compliant heart that is willing to submit, even when it doesn't agree. In fact, true submission doesn't even begin until agreement ends.

If an individual continually displays an unwilling and disobedient attitude, the mentor has no choice but to withdraw access and terminate the relationship. If this happens, it was not the mentor who broke the relationship — it was the one who chose rebellion and defiance.

Access cannot be granted to the disobedient. It would be insanity to reward a defiant attitude. The gift of access, placed into the wrong hands, becomes a deadly weapon used with crass insensitivity against the giver of the gift. The intimacy that was meant to bring sweet purity and perfume to the relationship now becomes defiled, perverted, and ravished. The knowledge that was given to equip is now used to compete. The secrets of the heart that were revealed in times of tenderness and warmth are now coldly falsified, twisted, and used to degrade, disgrace, and dishonor the mentor. The individual has revealed, by his disobedience, that he is not a protégé, but rather, a prodigal.

Many times in relationship, individuals really only want to talk about things as long as you're going to agree with them. They'll be excited to discuss the decisions that they've made, as long as they know you're going to agree. As a matter of fact, the prodigal is looking for the mentor to actually give him validation, so that *others* will agree with his decisions as well! Thoughts of submission and obedience are far from him.

> A PRODIGAL WANTS THE MENTOR TO EMBRACE AND APPROVE THE DECISIONS THAT HE HAS MADE;
>
> A PROTÉGÉ WANTS TO MAKE THE DECISIONS THAT ARE RECOMMENDED BY THE MENTOR.

If you ever have the audience of an individual that you respect, do not ask him a question and then disregard his advice, doing what you want to do anyway. Don't disrespect an individual so much that, *by your disobedient actions, you tell him,* "Your words meant absolutely nothing to me." Once that person finds out that you ignored the *gift of wisdom* that he extended to you, and that your own solution failed miserably, his response to you will be quite different the next time you seek his advice. Never be at a place where a future has been given to you, but you don't take it, due to disobedience. Obedience will open the doors to your future, while disobedience becomes the barred gates of a castle.

8. Desire to Please

A desire to please the one to whom you've been assigned is the eighth attribute that will qualify you for access. *People always gravitate toward the person who is trying to please them.* When you become passionate about pleasing those with whom you have relationship, you are paving the path to promotion and success.

People have this crazy idea that God does not want them to please men. But nothing could be further from the truth. I have heard many say, "I'm not a man-pleaser; I'm a God-pleaser!" I understand what they are saying, but I don't please a man for the sake of that man. I please man because that pleases God. Of course, I do this within the boundaries of integrity and Divine principle.

> PEOPLE ALWAYS GRAVITATE TOWARD THE PERSON WHO IS TRYING TO PLEASE THEM.

I chose long ago to please my superiors in everything. I want to be pleasing to them. I can't imagine them wanting me around, if I wasn't. I never want them to say, "Gosh, I wish you would do more!" Sometimes, we make the mistake of thinking that we only need to please God, not other people. But Godly principle says we must actually pursue obeying those who are over us in authority.[10] Now, you tell me, when we obey our authorities, is that bringing them pleasure? Certainly, but we are doing it as unto the Lord, and not man. This is something we must *deliberately choose* to do; pleasing others instead of ourselves certainly doesn't come naturally!

> A PRODIGAL CONCENTRATES ON SURPASSING THE MENTOR, WHILE A PROTÉGÉ CONCENTRATES ON PLEASING HIS MENTOR.

The primary aim of a prodigal is to do *whatever it takes* to get his agenda recognized and his abilities applauded. He is the type that will use and abuse others, in order to see his objective accomplished. He calculates that if he can play the 'good little protégé' game long enough, he can extract enough favor from the relationship to springboard himself to fame and fortune, leaving the mentor all alone. If a prodigal seeks to please his mentor at all, it is with the ulterior motive of stripping and surpassing him. He aims to take the wisdom gained through the intimacy of the relationship, and use it as strategy for his own personal gain and benefit.

---

10. See Ephesians 6:5

His pleasing attitude is not pure; it is tainted with the underlying greed for self-promotion.

But a true protégé recognizes his mentor as a valuable gift in his life, someone who can equip, motivate, and admonish him. He understands that his mentor can grant him favor and open doors of opportunity for him; but his attention and gratitude is not focused upon the favor and opportunities—it is focused on being pleasing to his mentor.

The greatest power gratitude possesses is its inability to remain hidden. Out of a heart brimming with gratitude, the protégé studies how he can please others. He does his research, so that he can surpass his mentor's expectations, before even being asked.

> THE GREATEST POWER GRATITUDE POSSESSES IS ITS INABILITY TO REMAIN HIDDEN.

He understands that when he joyfully gives his mentor *more* than he requires, he will be invited to a deeper level of intimacy. This deeper level of intimacy produces a deeper level of gratitude and commitment in the protégés heart, spurring him to find or invent more ways in which he can please his mentor. As this cycle repeats and accelerates, the relationship begins to generate its own synergy and creative power. Now, there is *nothing* that the mentor and protégé (father and son) cannot accomplish!

It's good and commendable to desire to please God. But, how can you please a God you can't see, if you can't please those whom you can see? When you seek to please those in authority, you are ultimately pleasing God as well.

9. Desire to Give

The attribute of giving is fundamental to healthy relationships. Motivational speaker Zig Ziglar frequently says, "You can have everything you want in life, if you help enough other people get what they want out of life." The concept he is talking about is one of having a heart and life that is focused on serving other people. The Bible puts it this way: *"Consider others' interests as more important than your own."*[11]

---

11. Philippians 2:4, author's paraphrase

> A PRODIGAL ASKS, "WHAT CAN I GET OUT OF THIS RELATIONSHIP?" A PROTÉGÉ PROCEEDS FROM "WHAT CAN I PUT INTO THIS RELATIONSHIP?" TO, "WHAT IS MY MENTOR GETTING OUT OF HIS RELATIONSHIP WITH ME?"

The desire to give is partnered with the desire to please. A grateful heart is the author of both desires, because gratitude for the blessings one has been given compels a person to give to others and to seek to please. Show me a stingy, selfish person, and I'll show you a person who has forsaken a grateful heart.

The first thought that enters the mind of most people, when faced with a new situation, is, "How is this going to affect *me?*" If they determine that they will be inconvenienced or required to do something unpleasant, they refuse to become involved. Sadly, we live in a very self-indulgent society, and even good people can become self-protective and tight-fisted with their time and resources.

A prodigal takes this selfishness one step further, and purposefully maneuvers to defraud someone. With a calculating and manipulative motive, he doesn't just aim for a "win-win" situation; he wants an "I win-you lose" outcome. *Giving* into the relationship doesn't even cross his mind. He's too consumed with his own self-importance.

The person that a mentor is searching for is someone who takes no thought

> WHAT YOU MAKE HAPPEN FOR SOMEONE ELSE, GOD WILL MAKE HAPPEN FOR YOU.

for himself, when confronted with new or challenging situations. He is looking for a protégé whose first impulse is to contribute and pour value into the situation— someone who is thinking about the cost to *others*, instead of the cost to himself.

Mentors and fathers are searching for cheerful *givers*, not stingy takers. Therefore understand *that what you make happen for someone else, God will make happen for you.*[12]

---

12. Mike Murdock, *My Personal Dream Book* (Denton, TX: The Wisdom Center, 2001), p. 22.

Choose to be a giver and find out what you can bring to the table, in your relationship with your mentors. Show yourself to be generous, and continually sow into their lives. Remember, the seed you sow today determines the future you will one day reap. Are you sowing into those who are going 'nowhere?' Or are you sowing into those who have been *where you want to go* and can help you get there? The seed of your life must be planted into the good soil of your mentor's life, if you ever desire to gain access.

10. Value

One of the most important things about building excellent relationships is realizing that other people are *valuable*. My focus should not be on how valuable I consider myself to be, and how I expect everyone else to appreciate my value. The Principle of Value tells me that *I need to value others*. I need to value their place, their position, and their contribution.

This is especially true as concerns those who are over me and have the responsibility of advising, warning, and correcting me. I must know who these people are in my life, and I must esteem them highly. Why? Because they are doing what nobody else wants to do! Therefore, I am going to respect them, even if I don't necessarily like them as people. I'm going to honor them, value them, and esteem them highly for the work that they do. In fact, these people are worthy of *double honor* in my life.

The Principle of Value, if honored, will protect your future. Whether you like to think about it or not, a day will come when you will be faced with a question that you cannot answer. If you've never sown into someone wise enough to answer that question, you'll have no help, you'll have no answer, and your life will take a downward spiral.

But, let's say that you *have* invested the time to recognize a mentor or a 'spiritual father,' and have pursued his wisdom and admonition. You've sown into his life and shown him value, respect, love, and faithfulness. You have reassured him of your servant's heart and proven your loyalty again and again, continually posturing as a student and a son, and demonstrating how important he is to you.

And now, your need comes to the surface. Your giant, the same one that he faced years ago, has now come. Do you think you'll have to fight that giant alone? Not a chance, because he will say, "Move out of the way, I'll take care of this one." Where did that favor and deliverance come from? It came from all of the sowing that you did! Because you esteemed your mentor, sowing dignity, respect, honor, and value into his life, he now becomes the hand of deliverance and favor in yours.

You must be ever mindful that there are situations in your future that will stop and destroy you, if you have not nurtured the value of key relationships in your life. For this very reason ancient kings made covenants with each other, and modern nations form alliances—because they knew that, at some point, they were going to come up against a common enemy.

Many people refuse to honor, refuse to esteem, and refuse to sow into the lives of others, because they think that it is, somehow, degrading. But do you understand that this is the reason why many of us feel so alone? *We haven't regarded others as being valuable.*

Embrace the Principle of Value in your relationships. Begin placing importance, value, and dignity on the lives of others. Until you recognize the *value* of a relationship, you will not be given *access* to a relationship.

WHY ACCESS REMAINS

To be *granted* access is one thing, but to *keep* the door of access open is a whole new challenge. Don't pursue access unless you are committed to *maintain* the relationship, for maintenance is, by far, the most difficult and crucial test of your commitment.

You must *continue to qualify* for your mentor's time. It is a sad and embarrassing day when I can no longer maintain a relationship that I worked so hard to enter. But, if I must ask to be released, I will do so, because I refuse to put my mentor in the difficult and uncomfortable position of continually having to adjust and correct me. By the same token, *I* must graciously release someone from a relationship with *me,* if he cannot maintain that level of intensity and mutual benefit.

There are countless factors involved in managing and maintaining an excellent relationship. The traits already discussed, which opened the door of access to you in the first place, must continue to grow and increase. And to these qualities many more are added, a few of which we will now discuss.

1. Faithfulness

Faithfulness is one of the most important qualities you can possess, in order to build solid relationships. If you are faithful, you never need to wonder whether or not you will remain in relationship with those who invited you into their life. Your relationship will remain intact as long as you remain faithful. I find it sadly amusing when I hear someone say, "I was faithful for ten years." Well, all you're telling me by that statement is that now you're no longer faithful.

Jesus said that if you are faithful with what belongs to another man, you will someday have your own. He also said if you're unfaithful over little, you will be denied access to more.[13] The day you jump out of faithfulness is the day that you now have become unfaithful.

Faithfulness is a virtue that is only proven at the end of one's life. Let me give you an example: a husband tells the counselor, "I have been faithful to my wife—six days this week I focused on her and loved

> HE WHO CEASES TO REMAIN FAITHFUL PROVES HE TRULY NEVER WAS.

her. There was just one night I was with another woman." Now you tell me, was he faithful? Of course not! Neither are we, unless we *continue* to be faithful until our last day. *He who ceases to remain faithful proves he truly never was.*

Faithfulness means that when I am asked to adjust or change something, I don't ignore, disregard, or forget that it needs to be done. I get busy and do it, without it having to be brought to me again. Relationships can never grow or get any better if the same issues have to be addressed over and over.

---

13. See Luke 16:10-12

Solomon once asked, *"Most men will proclaim each his own goodness, but* **who can find a faithful man?"**[14] That's a very good question—one that many employers, mentors, fathers, and spouses are constantly asking! Faithfulness will take you further than your talent ever will. I know some people who are very talented. These individuals are great at what they do, but I can't get them to do what needs to be done. They don't keep their word, and never finish what they've started. Not once does Divine instruction say that leaders are to commit anything to those who are *skillful.* Instead, the apostle Paul instructs Timothy, *"And the things that you have heard from me among many witnesses, commit these to* **faithful** *men, who will be able to teach others also."*[15]

Access remains as long as we are faithful to *continue.* When we *continue* to respect and grow and honor and please, we are being faithful to the gratitude that must be shown for the marvelous privilege of relationship

2. Kindness

Kindness is an essential ingredient in any relationship. When intimacy crosses over the line of familiarity, unkindness and disrespect often follow. To continue to be kind requires that you become understanding. Even after you've learned all of a person's little, irritating idiosyncrasies (or sometimes big, glaring idiosyncrasies!), make a point to express genuine kindness toward them.

To be kind does not mean that you have to agree with any wrongdoing. It means that you assume a posture of compassion. When someone is struggling with something, you can let him or her know, "I understand. It's okay. Don't worry about it. We're going to make it through this."

Kindness takes discipline, because many times we may not feel like being kind. It is your responsibility to monitor your heart and to control your tongue. If you don't put a muzzle on yourself, you could easily react with foolish and hurtful words. The moment that you don't discipline yourself, your relationships are going to pay for it.

A young lady by the name of Ruth once discovered how quickly this quality of kindness would unlock doors to one's future. In giving honor, respect, and

14. Proverbs 20:6
15. 2 Timothy 2:2

kindness to Boaz, a man of wealth and influence in his community, she opened the door to her destiny. Boaz's response to her was full of favor, *"And now, my daughter, fear not. I will do for you all you require, for all my people in the city know that you are a woman of strength, worth, bravery, [and] capability."*[16]

Do you have relationships with people who seem unresponsive and unpleasant? Honey attracts much more effectively than vinegar. You can slide a lot farther on grease than you can on cinders! Drop any poor attitudes that you may be harboring, go the extra mile, and be kind toward people.

> YOUR DESTINY IS BIRTHED THE MOMENT YOU SOW YOURSELF INTO ANOTHER MAN'S LIFE.

Try a little kindness and understanding, and see what happens. Don't be surprised if your kindness eventually evokes a very pleasant response from even the most unresponsive. Boaz responded with these words, "All that you require I will do for you. Everything you want. Anything, you name it. It's yours. Everything you require, I'll do." Kindness is the reason Ruth ended up in the genealogy of Jesus. She found her destiny and her purpose, because she demonstrated kindness, without compromising her character. *Your destiny is birthed the moment you sow yourself into another man's life.*

3. Loyalty

Loyalty is simply an unswerving commitment to another. It is a sorely missing element in many relationships today. We have forgotten what it means to be loyal. Our consumer mentality has contributed to this, to some degree. People are no longer loyal to a product. And unfortunately, many companies are not loyal to their clients or patrons. This penchant for disloyalty has poured over into the arena of relationships.

It is one thing to switch brands of dishwashing detergent. It is another thing altogether to switch friends, or pastors, or spouses. Sometimes we just need to be loyal, and let the relationship move forward. We need a higher level of stick-to-it type attitudes!

---

16. Ruth 3:11, *AMP*

This kind of 'stubborn loyalty' will take your relationships to a much deeper level. *Loyalty is never as beautiful as the day that betrayal rears its ugly head.*

What a powerful thing it is for a mentor to know he has a relationship with someone who is profoundly loyal to him, knowing that neither of you are going to split, when things get tough.

> LOYALTY IS NEVER AS BEAUTIFUL AS THE DAY THAT BETRAYAL REARS ITS UGLY HEAD.

So many times, people do not remain loyal to the commitments they made to others. Respectfully, I can probably count on one hand the number of individuals who have proven their loyalty to me. You may say, "I have a lot of friends that are loyal." But, I can assure you of this—your standards have been lowered, in order to make that happen. Successful relationships are those with longevity of commitment—the choice to remain through the tough times, as well as the good times.

Longevity of commitment is an earmark of a protégé. He is preparing for a future that will bring honor and fulfillment not only to him, but also to his mentor. The prodigal, on the other hand, is looking to defraud; he wants to pilfer every advantage that he can get, before *exiting* the relationship. *He was disloyal in his heart, long before his feet ever walked out the door.*

Too many people abandon and desert their places of transformative growth, because of hard times. I believe that we become better people by remaining loyal. Although it may *seem* like your mentor was not loyal to you, this does not mean that you now have the right to become disloyal to him. There is something good that comes from sticking it out. Now obviously, I'm not saying to support harmful or illegal behavior; that would be a different subject and would require different guidelines. But in general, when times are hard, be loyal. When others aren't, be loyal.

Loyalty is absolute. It is the basic requirement for relationship. The painful wounds of disloyalty pierce deeper and produce more agony than perhaps any other form of disrespect known to man. Loyalty does not come in degrees. There is no such thing as being 'somewhat loyal.' (That is as ridiculous as saying that one can be 'somewhat pregnant!') You are either loyal or disloyal. There is no middle ground.

A person who is truly loyal is *openly* loyal. If you will not publicly defend and protect your mentor when he or she is absent, then you cannot call yourself loyal. You have no right to expect access into the life of anyone that you are unwilling to *openly* guard and protect.

4. Protection

Love is confirmed by the willingness to protect those around you. If you genuinely love, respect, and honor someone, you will demonstrate it by your willingness to protect them, both privately and publicly.

The door of access will not be held open long to a person who will not protect, for *to not protect is to become a danger and a threat.* Intimacy requires that one can let down his guard, knowing that the relationship is a safe, secure place, where his needs can be met and he can be refreshed. This kind of transparency and vulnerability is possible only when an individual knows he is protected.

> A PRODIGAL BELIEVES THAT THE MENTOR SHOULD PROTECT HIM; A PROTÉGÉ BELIEVES THAT HE SHOULD PROTECT THE MENTOR.

One of the greatest things that you can ever do for a mentor in your life is to protect him, because when you're protecting him, you're really protecting your own future. If you don't protect him, you have sabotaged everything you say that you believe. You have planted a seed that will ultimately abort your future.

It is never the mentor's responsibility to protect himself. It is always the protégé's responsibility to protect the mentor. David, the Israelite king of old acknowledged this:

> Lo, children are an heritage of the LORD: and the fruit of the womb is his reward. As arrows are in the hand of a mighty man; so are children of the youth. Happy is the man that hath his quiver full of them: they shall not be ashamed, but they shall speak with the enemies in the gate.[17]

17. Psalm 127:3-5, *KJV*

The *sons* are the ones that speak to the enemy, *not the father.* The only way to see reward come from your relationship with your mentor is to aggressively protect him. You'll never gain the access that you desire without protecting him. You'll never gain the position of trust that you desire, if you cannot be trusted to protect. You'll never partake of the jewels of wisdom that God has placed in the heart of your mentor or father, if he ever suspects that you possess the spirit of a betrayer. And you'll never receive the future God has for you, if you do not protect *your father's future.*

5. Humility

Jesus had this to say about humility, *"...whoever humbles himself as this little child is the greatest in the kingdom of heaven."*[18] Humility is having a clear understanding of who you *are* and who you are *not* in any given relationship. Humility will always cause you to posture yourself correctly, and it will dispel all presumptive attitudes, causing an attitude of thankfulness to flourish. *It is important to recognize who you are, but it is more important to acknowledge who you are not.*

> IT IS IMPORTANT TO RECOGNIZE WHO YOU ARE, BUT IT IS MORE IMPORTANT TO ACKNOWLEDGE WHO YOU ARE NOT.

Humility will always capture the heart of the one you love and desire to serve. It will keep your heart tender and moldable, easily instructed and corrected. Humility will cause you to be a self-corrector. When correction from another is necessary, your quick admission of wrong will immediately stop prosecution and bring restoration of fellowship to the relationship.

Humility will keep your heart tender toward your mentor's guidance. One of the most enlightening yet ironic truths that humility has taught me is that when *I thought* I was ready and qualified to do something, I never was. And when I was sure that I was *not* ready for the task, and I didn't even *want* to do it, that is when my authority said I was actually qualified!

Humility is the quality that has helped me to maintain the relationships that I have been granted access to. It will one day bring me honor, for God says humility must come before honor.

---

18. Matthew 18:4

6. Discretion

Your access to great people will remain only as long as you understand discretion. I cannot express to you the importance of understanding discretion. The Psalmist wrote, *"A good man shows favor and lends. He is gracious and full of compassion. **He guides his affairs with discretion.**"*[19]

A person of discretion relates to people judiciously, which means he exercises good judgment in matters of protocol and appropriate behavior. He knows when to talk and when to attentively listen. He can be trusted to keep a confidence and to protect others in his conversation.

A person of discretion understands timing. He knows that even the right thing at the wrong time is the wrong thing. He is sensitive to a person's receptivity. He listens to what a person doesn't say, just as carefully as he listens to what is said.

A discreet individual has a quick, intuitive appreciation for what is fit, proper, and right in any situation. His words are spoken with tact, and he is especially skilled in sensing and avoiding what would offend or disturb. If disturbing words must be spoken, he knows how to communicate them with grace and kindness, for *"faithful are the wounds of a friend…"*[20] He guides all of his affairs and conversations with caution, prudence, and restraint.

Very few qualities will give you access quicker than discretion. And nothing will remove favor from your life faster than a lack of it.

These qualities extend into all of the character issues of life, and will dictate whether or not you will be given entrance to the lives of those who can change your future. There is someone watching you at all times, waiting to see if you will posture correctly and pursue passionately. Many are *called* to pursue. Very few do. Will you be one of the few? Will you embrace the Law of Access? My prayer is that you do.

---

19. Psalm 112:4-5, author's paraphrase
20. Proverbs 27:6

THE LAW OF ACCESS

There are unspoken rules
both to access and to remain in relationship.

- → A broken heart is the fruit of an unscrupulous relationship.
- → You will suffer both the consequences and the rewards of those who are closest to you.
- → *Protocol* is a term given to the rules that govern how to enter and how to remain in any relationship.
- → Never allow the invitation of intimacy to be destroyed by the contempt of familiarity.
- → Only when I have properly postured myself am I able to truly give or receive in relationship.
- → Future access will always be granted the moment you choose to bring pleasure to those who are important to your life.
- → Every relationship feeds a strength or a weakness within you.
- → A prodigal wants the mentor to pursue him; a protégé makes it his aim to pursue his mentor.
- → The reward of any relationship is determined by the value that is placed upon it.
- → Respect is magnetic. It will attract people, while disrespect will repel them.
- → A prodigal respects with his words, but not with his heart; a protégé lets his actions be the spokesman of his heart.
- → Respect is the key that opens the door of access.
- → Don't relate to people through God, but relate to God through people.
- → Honor is the gate through which all Godly relationships enter.
- → Joy must be the attitude of choice long before you know the outcome of your circumstances.
- → Your *attitude* in life will determine your *altitude* in life.

+ A true servant gladly abandons all personal pleasure, in order to become a tool in the hand of the one he serves.

+ A prodigal is interested in the details of his own life; a protégé is interested in the details of another's.

+ Immediate attention to detail gets the immediate attention of the one whom you seek to please.

+ A prodigal wants to exploit the mentor's gifts and skills to become great; a protégé wants to develop his gifts and skills to the end that his mentor would be great.

+ The crown of a man's character and purpose is born the moment he realizes his duty to obey.

+ A prodigal wants the mentor to embrace and approve the decisions that he has made; a protégé wants to make the decisions that are recommended by the mentor.

+ People always gravitate toward the person who is trying to please them.

+ A prodigal concentrates on surpassing the mentor, while a protégé concentrates on pleasing his mentor.

+ The greatest power gratitude possesses is its inability to remain hidden.

+ A prodigal asks, "What can I get out of this relationship?" A protégé proceeds from, "What can I put into this relationship?" to "What is my mentor getting out his relationship with me?"

+ What you make happen for someone else, God will make happen for you.

+ He who ceases to remain faithful proves he truly never was.

+ Your destiny is birthed the moment you sow yourself into another man's life.

+ Loyalty is never as beautiful as the day that betrayal rears its ugly head.

+ A prodigal believes that the mentor should protect him; a protégé believes that he should protect the mentor.

+ It is important to recognize who you are, but it is more important to acknowledge who you are not.

THE LAW OF
COVENANT

The mark of a healthy relationship is security, which is a result of trust.

3

THE MARK OF

A HEALTHY RELATIONSHIP IS SECURITY,

WHICH IS A RESULT OF TRUST.

In other words: If you are in a relationship where you constantly have to look over your shoulder, get out! You are in the wrong relationship! This law introduces the concept of covenant. Good relationships may begin because of common purpose, mutual support, and so forth, but they *endure* because of commitment and covenant. What exactly do I mean by covenant?

COVENANT

Modern society, for the most part, is sorely bereft of understanding in matters of covenant. The blatant evidence of this ignorance is displayed daily in courtrooms, businesses, churches, and homes all over the world. Transience, rather than longevity, is the order of the day. In our spiritually bankrupt Western culture for example, it is common for people to hire lawyers to help them find a way to *break* their word or commitment, rather than keep it.

The Hebrew word for covenant is *beriyth*, which means "a cutting," or "a compact made by passing between two pieces of flesh." It is similar to the ancient Assyrian word, *biritu*, which means "fetter, chain" or "to bind," the covenant being that which binds together the parties who enter such an agreement.

The phrase "cutting a covenant" is derived after an ancient custom, where an agreement between two parties was confirmed by slaughtering and cutting an animal into two halves. Each party would pass between the two pieces, pledging his faithfulness to the covenant. This ceremony signified that if either of them were unfaithful and broke the covenant, his life would be destroyed, as was the slain and divided beast.[1]

In essence, a covenant is an agreement, but a *serious* agreement of a solemn and binding force. It is an agreement between two people that involves *promises and requirements* on the part of each to the other. Each party is binding him or herself to fulfill certain conditions, while also being assured of certain privileges.

In biblical covenants, God was solemnly invoked as a witness to the covenant, and an oath (a promise to keep the agreement) was sworn.[2] This calling upon God as a witness explains, for example, why the marriage contract is called "...the covenant of...God."[3] Because the unchanging, eternal God was the witness to every type of covenant, *a breach of covenant was regarded as a heinous sin.*[4]

In its earliest form, covenant established a *blood brotherhood*, in which two men became brothers by drinking each other's blood. Ordinarily, this meant that one was adopted into the clan of the other. The establishment of a covenant bound an individual not only to his new blood-brother, but also to his brother's family, his community, and his gods. In this early idea, then, the covenant was not a mere alliance made to gain certain goods or advantages. Rather, it was a *sacred declaration of fidelity.* It bound the parties together not only in material goods, but also in every other arena of life. In later covenants, there were various substitutes

1. See Genesis 15:9-10, 17-18; Jeremiah 34:18-20
2. See Genesis 21:3
3. Proverbs 2:17
4. See Ezekiel 17:12-20

for the drinking of each other's blood, namely, drinking together the animal's sacrificial blood, sprinkling it upon the parties, eating a sacrificial meal together, and so on. All these methods were used to express the same idea—*the fettering together of lives,* resulting from a covenant.[5]

Because of the serious, life-altering implications surrounding the making of a covenant, these agreements were entered into with solemn ceremony. Usually, covenant making involved the following principle elements:[6]

- **A statement of the terms agreed upon**[7]—The terms of the covenant were clearly laid out and always all-inclusive.
- **An oath by each party to observe the terms, God being witness of the oath**[8]—The oath was such a characteristic feature, that sometimes the term "oath" is used interchangeably with the term "covenant."
- **A curse invoked by each one upon himself, in the event that he broke the agreement.**—In a sense this may be considered a part of the oath, adding emphasis to it. This curse was usually not explicitly stated in the case of human covenants, but was inferred in covenants between God and man.[9]
- **The formal ratification of the covenant by some solemn external act.**— It is by this act that the covenant was "sealed." The different ceremonies for this "sealing" could included:
  - Sprinkling of the sacrificed animal's blood upon both parties
  - Eating a common meal
  - Sharing grains of salt—"A covenant of salt," as it was called, originated in eastern cultures. It was also called the covenant of friendship, thus the phrase "to eat salt together." Salt, the antidote to corruption, was used in every sacrifice to denote purity and perpetuity. So a perpetual, everlasting covenant was often "sealed" with salt.[10]
  - A material pledge
  - The presentation of a gift
  - Setting up a monument, such as a heap of stones

5. *International Standard Bible Encyclopedia,* Electronic Database Copyright (c)1996 by Biblesoft.
6. Ibid.
7. See Genesis 26:28-29; 31:50-52
8. See Genesis 26:31; 31:48-53
9. See Deuteronomy 27:15-26
10. *Fausset's Bible Dictionary,* Electronic Database Copyright (c)1998 by Biblesoft.

CONDITIONS AND PROMISES

Covenant is two-sided. It involves *both* individuals putting something into the relationship. Covenant is conditional. In order to be a beneficiary of the *advantages* of the covenant relationship, each party must fulfill the *obligatory requirements* of the relationship. *To seek the benefits (promises) of a covenant without meeting the conditions is considered a breach of the covenant.*

> TO SEEK
>
> THE BENEFITS (PROMISES)
>
> OF A COVENANT WITHOUT
>
> MEETING THE CONDITIONS
>
> IS CONSIDERED A
>
> BREACH OF THE COVENANT.

Let's look at some examples of biblical covenants, and examine the conditions and promises behind them.

God With Abraham

The condition of this covenant was that Abram must leave his country, kindred, and father's house. He was to follow the Lord into the land that He would show him. In return, God promised him increase and a great line of descendants. He said, *"...I will bless you and make your name great..."*[11]

About fourteen years later, this covenant was renewed and ratified when God changed Abram's name to Abraham and established circumcision as a sign.[12]

God With Israel

The condition of this covenant was that the Israelites accept, keep, and obey the words of God, as found in the Ten Commandments. In return, God promised to bless Israel with protection, provision, and prosperity. They would enjoy victory over their enemies and experience the outpouring of His Spirit.[13] As with Abraham, this covenant was ratified and "sealed" by circumcision.[14]

David And Jonathan

David and Jonathan made a covenant of *mutual protection* that would be binding on their descendants forever.[15]

11. Genesis 12:2
12. See Genesis 17
13. See Exodus 23:20-33
14. See Deuteronomy 10:16
15. See 1 Samuel 18:3; 20:8, 16-18, 42; 2 Samuel 9

God And Mankind

God's covenant with mankind is one of love and loyalty. It is somewhat different because it is a *covenant of grace*. It was God's grace through Jesus' life, ministry, death, and resurrection, and not man's response, that ratified this covenant. God guaranteed that He would provide salvation, in spite of man's inability (because of his sin) to keep his side of the covenant.

The benefits of this covenant are almost too marvelous to describe. Through this covenant, believers are justified by God's grace and mercy rather than their own human attempts to keep the law. They obtain forgiveness of sins, a *personal relationship* with God, and eternal life in heaven. They have the power to live free from wrongdoing, and to walk in Divine wholeness in body, mind, and spirit. They can enjoy material, emotional, relational, and spiritual prosperity. Through His Spirit, they have peace, joy, life, love, and many more benefits, too numerous to list. What a powerful covenant!

Although this is a covenant of grace, it is nonetheless a covenant, and like any covenant, *it is conditional*. The condition is that those who enter this covenant repent of their sin and put their faith in the personal saving power of Jesus' death, burial, and resurrection. Then, they are expected to express this faith through a grateful and obedient lifestyle.

MORE THAN AN AGREEMENT

Let's look at the definition of this Law of Covenant again. It states: The mark of a healthy relationship is *security*, which is a result of trust. Why is this true? Security is possible because a covenant is something much more binding than a mere contract or agreement. Let me give you three distinct differences between a contract and a covenant:

- ❖ **Duration**—A contract always has an end date, while a covenant is a *permanent* arrangement. Covenants are lifelong commitments.

✦ **All-inclusive**—By all-inclusive, I mean that a covenant involves all of you. Whereas a contract generally involves only one part of a person, such as a skill, a covenant covers a *person's total being*.[16]

✦ **Written on the heart**—A contract is usually written on paper, with built-in loopholes, depending on the shrewdness of its architects. Conversely, a covenant is not written with ink on paper, but rather, with spirit, upon human hearts.

There is nothing as binding nor as fulfilling as a covenant relationship. People who have covenanted together are committed to do whatever it takes to preserve the longevity and value of their relationship. They go through hard years together. They endure the pain of character-building seasons with each other.

These are not the superficial friendships, acquaintances, and "arrangements" so common in today's world. The concept of covenant is understood by very few. True covenant requires integrity, generosity, loyalty, and the demonstration of a selfless character, all qualities of which our society is painfully deficient.

A DESTITUTE GENERATION

Even though the 60's and 70's generation was very rebellious and largely independent, the present generation is downright recalcitrant and crudely individualistic. They are isolationists who love to sit for hours in front of their computers, talking only by words typed on a screen. Many have no real relationships, since they only relate electronically. They have little interest in commitment, accountability, or covenant. Consequently, they have become a generation of self-centered people. With such people at the

> THE MOST ACCURATE TEST OF CHARACTER OCCURS WHEN WE ARE THROWN INTO THE LION'S DEN OF HUMANITY.

16. *Nelson's Illustrated Bible Dictionary,* Copyright (c)1986, Thomas Nelson Publishers.

reigns of global leadership, I predict that the world faces a tremendous challenge in the days ahead.

Character cannot be tested in isolation. Virtue cannot be developed nor proven through text messaging. Growth and maturity can only come when people are forced to interact face to face, through committed relationships. *The most accurate test of character occurs when we are thrown into the lion's den of humanity.*

THE CHARACTER OF COVENANT

My ability to keep covenant with you is not dependent on *your* character, but upon *my* character. *Character ensures the integrity of any covenant.* Lack of character is the reason that so many people have repeated 'miscarriages' in the arena of relationships. They just don't know how to stay and complete—to stick it out, even through relational adversity!

> CHARACTER ENSURES
> THE INTEGRITY
> OF ANY COVENANT.

What type of character, attitude, and demeanor is exhibited by someone who has committed himself to a covenant relationship? What are the unquestioned "givens" that form the secure bedrock of such a relationship?

Firstly, there must be a commitment to "Lock In". There is no real value in transient relationships. What happens so frequently is that people jump into relationships from a short-term perspective. Don't rush! Take your time and assess the prospective relationship. If you decide that you want to walk with that individual on a long-term basis, say, "OK, this is it, I'm locking in." Until you lock into a relationship, there can be no benefit for either party.

After locking into relationship with her mother-in-law, Ruth declared, *"Don't ask me to leave you and turn back. I will go wherever you go and live wherever you* live. *Your people will be my people, and your God will be my God. I will die where you die and will be buried there. May the Lord punish me severely if I allow anything but death to separate us!"* [17] Ruth made a choice to walk in covenant with her mentor.

It is pointless to make *temporal choices* based on ever-changing circumstances. Individuals continually approach their relationships one day at a time, making decisions as situations arise. You'll get more out of focusing on the good parts of a challenging, *committed* relationship than you would ever get from an easy, yet uncommitted relationship.

Sadly, most people prefer *periodical friendships* to lifelong covenant commitments. Your relationships must *deepen* as time goes on. Ultimately, that is the only way that they will produce the kind of life that you want to enjoy. Never be ashamed of caring too much, or of holding people to their commitments. This is the foundation of covenant relationship.

What's Mine is Yours

The essence of covenant relationship is mutual reliance and interdependence. *By personal choice,* each party brings to the relationship all that he has, ready to contribute to the hopes, dreams, and future of his partner.

It is important to note that this sharing of resources, whether material goods, favor, or wisdom is not the result of some sort of "commune" mentality. The purpose of covenant is *not* to level the playing field, or to fleece the "haves" to give to the "have-nots." That is what I would call a "prodigal's mind-set."

A prodigal doesn't give anyone the chance to *choose* to give—he's already got his hand out, impatiently sputtering the words of cloaked begging! The prodigal feels that he is *entitled* to the resources of another, and if the response is not as generous as he expected, he becomes indignant and angry.

In contrast, the person in covenant is focused on contributing what he can to

---

17. Ruth 1:16-17, *NLT*; Ruth was a young lady from the ancient country of Moab. She spoke this oath to her mother-in-law, Naomi.

the relationship—he is not calculating how he can gain an advantage. When resources are given and privileges extended, he responds with profound gratitude.

The most important thing to remember is that *no one owes us anything,* no matter how close and intimate the relationship. By keeping a consistently grateful posture, you give your covenant partner the *joy of initiating* when and how he wants to bless you.

When you enter into a covenant relationship, position yourself as the giver in the relationship, not the receiver.

> THE PRODIGAL FEELS THAT HE IS *ENTITLED* TO THE RESOURCES OF ANOTHER, WHILE THE PROTÉGÉ RESPONDS TO WHATEVER HE RECEIVES WITH HEARTFELT GRATITUDE.

Understand that the relationship is not a give and take arrangement—it is a *give* arrangement! Becoming a giver in relationship is not a result of what you do—*it's who you are.* Givers give, in the same way that painters paint, singers sing, or farmers farm! The automatic response of a grateful heart is to give.

A covenant relationship is *not a partnership.* A 50/50 partnership is usually set up with each partner contributing part of what they have, to make up the whole. A covenant relationship, however, is a 100/100 arrangement. Each party enters the arena ready to contribute 100% to the success of the relationship, eager to give 100% of their life to promote the other's future and dreams. When *both parties* enter the relationship in this manner, *everyone's* needs get met, and *everyone's* future is bright!

CONTRIBUTE, DON'T COMPETE

In the companionship of covenant, you must each bring to the relationship elements that the other needs. One contributes what the other lacks. Your strengths cover the other's weaknesses. This is why the *Principle of Difference* is so important. *It states: Your value in any relationship is determined by your diversity.*

> YOUR VALUE IN ANY RELATIONSHIP IS DETERMINED BY YOUR DIVERSITY.

Ask yourself this question: What do I bring to the table that no one else brings? I learned long ago to quit competing with people. I always take time to carefully watch those I am in covenant relationship with. I observe what their strong points are, and I stay away from those strengths; in areas where they are strong, they don't need me. Instead, I fill in the cavities of their weaknesses, thus becoming what they need. And when you are in a person's life to meet *his* needs and add value to *him*, God finds someone to meet your needs and bring value to *you*.

Contrary to popular opinion, your value and weight in any relationship is not obtained by demanding your 'rights,' or rising up and proclaiming, "Well that's just the way I am. You need to accept me for who I am!" Your value in any rela-

> YOUR VALUE IN ANY RELATIONSHIP IS THE *DIFFERENCE* THAT YOU CAN BRING, TO CAUSE SUCCESS TO COME TO YOUR FRIEND.

tionship is the *difference* that you can bring, to cause success to come to your friend. When we choose to become what we need to be for someone else, our value and influence soar.

Now, I don't choose to become what other people need because I'm afraid of what may happen if I don't. I am not passively allowing myself to be molded by another person. I become what is necessary, because I realize that doing so gives me a real reason to be in that relationship. I've earned my position at any table, the moment that I become what someone needs me to become. I am the one they are looking for, because I have answers and solutions to their problems. You must understand that *your value to others is in direct proportion to the problems you solve for them.*

Many people become very frustrated in life because they don't see a purpose in what they are doing. They feel valueless and unappreciated. Remember, you will be needed in *every* relationship, when you are willing to lay down what you perceive to be your own identity, and you embrace the identity that's necessary. Become what another needs. Answer questions that no one else can answer. Keep promises that

> YOUR VALUE TO OTHERS
> IS IN DIRECT PROPORTION
> TO THE PROBLEMS
> YOU SOLVE FOR THEM.

others break. Be willing to go where no one else will go. Be willing to do what no one else will do, and do it well.

This unselfish posturing is a rare and priceless quality, and it will be the difference that opens doors for you. What do you bring to the table that another person doesn't bring? If you ever want to be someone that others can't live without, demonstrate your *differences* not your similarities.

One of the greatest things that you can ever do with your life is to learn how to make and keep promises to people. People have the idea that if they don't make promises, they won't break promises, but that's

> A COVENANT
> NOT MADE IS A COVENANT
> NOT ENJOYED.

not true. *A covenant not made is a covenant not enjoyed.* I can never enjoy a covenant that I refuse to make. If I'm not willing to make a promise, I'll never be able to savor the benefits of commitment.

I enjoy making promises to people because it shows me who I am. If I make no promises, I live without an identity. The moment that I make a promise and keep my promise, I begin to gain an identity; it shows me that the promise-keeping God is alive inside of me. God never, ever, *ever* makes a promise that He doesn't keep.

MUTUAL COVENANT DECLARATIONS

As I mentioned earlier, sometimes the term "oath" is used in place of the term "covenant." Remember, that every covenant relationship will bring its own unique conditions and promises, and therefore, its own unique oaths. But I would like to share with you some declarations that are essential and foundational to *all* covenant relationships:

1. The Oath to Keep God In The Center

It is important that *both* of you trust God to be the witness and the preserver of your mutual covenant. The covenant relationship you have made with each other becomes susceptible to rupture, if you haven't invited Someone greater than both of you to protect and guard it. I see this happen in marriages all the time, but it is just as true in other covenantal relationships.

The Law of Covenant requires that each individual be compelled, *by their own personal covenant with God,* to fulfill the conditions and obligations of the human covenant. *Remember, to expect the promises and benefits of covenant, without fulfilling the conditions and requirements of covenant, is actually a breach of covenant.* When I keep my covenant with you, I am keeping my covenant with God. If I break covenant with you, I have also broken covenant with God.

2. The Pledge to Protect

The evidence of love is the pledge to protect. A person will risk his goods, his reputation, and even his life to protect what he loves. The most effective protection is produced through partnership. It is very difficult to protect someone who doesn't want to be protected. It is impossible to protect someone who interprets your protection as an attempt to stifle or control.

Let's again talk about the relationship between a mentor and a protégé, for a moment. Quite often, the protégé who is not in covenant with his mentor sees the mentor's restraint as control, to hold him to the past. However, the protégé who has a covenant relationship with his mentor sees the mentor's restraint as wisdom, to protect his future. He understands that the mentor will do everything he can to stop his protégé from doing the wrong thing. He will warn him, he will throw *himself* down on the railroad tracks! He will do

> THE EVIDENCE OF LOVE IS THE PLEDGE TO PROTECT.

anything to try to prevent his protégé from making a decision that will ruin his future.

Actually, the only difference between control and correction lies in the heart of the receiver. *Without covenant*, the protégé will likely think that the mentor's purpose, in restraining him, is to hold him back from opportunity and promotion. At that point, the mentor has no choice but to back off. The most grievous aspect of this scenario is that after the deceived protégé disregards all warnings, forges ahead with his destructive behavior, and begins to reap the negative consequences, he angrily blames the mentor for all of his misfortune. I see this quite often.

> THE ONLY DIFFERENCE BETWEEN CONTROL AND CORRECTION LIES IN THE HEART OF THE RECEIVER.

By contrast, the protégé *in covenant* heeds his mentor's warnings, recognizing those admonitions as God's protective voice in his life. His heart is grateful that God has placed someone in his life to guard and watch over his future, and he is quick to embrace the wisdom of his authority.

This principle is true in all covenant relationships. Covenant always implies a pledge to protect, no matter what.

3. The Promise of Truth

Consider this: *"A friend loves at all times and a brother is born for adversity."*[18] Do you know that although a friend loves at all times, a true friend does not accept everything that you do? Remember this: *"Faithful are the wounds of a friend."*[19] A real friend will love you, but he will still tell you the truth. In fact, it is *because* he loves you, that he will tell you the truth.

Whether your attitudes and actions are constructive or destructive, they will all bring *consequences* to your life. Everything in life has consequences. Every relationship has consequences. But, when people make unwise choices, they often want mercy introduced into their situations. They think that mercy can abort destructive consequences. They believe that mercy means, "I can do what I want to do, and you will still accept me."

18. Proverbs 17:17
19. Proverbs 27:6

We must remember something. *God is merciful. He always accepts us, no matter how far we have fallen.* But interestingly, *He never approves of our wrongdoing.* An erroneous understanding of mercy, many times, becomes the door that introduces broken covenant in relationship. Some think that mercy says, "Withhold the truth concerning this subject, because you need to love this person through something." Friend, this is not mercy!

The purest form of mercy is when you love someone enough to tell him the truth. Genuine mercy will be quick to *protect a brother's future,* even if it means the uncomfortable task of telling him the truth today. Mercy will honor the covenantal pledge of protection, while remaining ever truthful.

This does not mean you become a critic. There's a big difference between speaking the truth in love, and criticizing. Criticism is your quickest way to loneliness, for soon no one will be good enough for you. Lonely people can have a house full of people and still be lonely.

You have to fight tirelessly for those in covenant with you. You must fight to prevent them from falling the first time, because if they fall too far and too hard, they may never recover. A person who understands covenant will fight for the future of his partner, when his partner has opened the door to compromise. He does not placate his friend's bad choices with mindless words of affirmation, by saying, "Oh, brother, I love you. Don't worry about it. It'll be OK. You know, God loves you." Remember, he might not really know what's wrong in his life, until you tell him what's wrong, or until somebody loves him enough to tell him the truth.

A covenant partner will risk rejection to tell you the truth. He will remind you of the standard of truth that both of you previously agreed upon. Truth is a standard; truth is a rule. It is correctness, and it is accuracy. Truth suggests conformity with the facts. Truth is habitual adherence to the same.

To live with no standard of truth is to attempt to go through life walking on quicksand. How can you go anywhere in life if, in fact, you have no standard to hold yourself to, no way to measure *real truth?* Every person alive acts according to what *they believe* the truth really is. Everyone does that; they believe that it's the truth and that's why they do it. But, truth is not according to the way that *I* see it or the way that *you* see it. Truth is according to the way that *God* sees it.

Once again, lets read this powerful verse: *"Faithful are the wounds of a friend; but the kisses of an enemy are deceitful."*[20] A faithful friend is not one who constantly tells you how wonderful you are. Rather, it is he who will face off with you about your shortcomings. Now, remember what's good for the goose is good for the gander, right? So I can't expect to have the freedom to tell someone else the truth, if I'm not willing to receive the truth about my own shortcomings.

If I haven't done what I am supposed to do, then you have a love-covenant obligation to come to me. Divine principle says that if your brother offends you, you are to *go to him*. Don't talk about him. Don't storm out of his life. *Go to him.* Fight for the life of your partner. If you really love him, you will not just sit by and let him err. You will be faithful. You will get in his face and tell him the truth—because that's what the law of covenant calls you to do.

4. The Vow to Never Leave

How can a person make this vow? The assurance of this solemn oath is contained in the pure and unselfish *motive* of true covenant. Here is a powerful principle: *The manner in which you treat a relationship when you no longer need it reveals the motive you had for it from the beginning.*

> THE MANNER IN WHICH YOU TREAT A RELATIONSHIP WHEN YOU NO LONGER NEED IT REVEALS THE MOTIVE YOU HAD FOR IT FROM THE BEGINNING.

The way that you treat a relationship, when it no longer saves your life, pays your bills, or soothes your broken heart, reveals the motive that you had for it, from the very beginning. It is impossible to escape your motives.

Carefully examine your motives before entering any relationship, but especially a covenant relationship. If there is even a shred of selfishness in your heart, any thought of, "What's in it for me?" you would be wise to stop pursuing that

20. Proverbs 27:6

relationship until you purify your motives. If you forge ahead, with selfishness in your heart, it will be worse for you than if you had never entered that covenant relationship. Peter said the second state of the man is worse than the beginning, *"For it would have been better for them not to have known the way of righteousness, than having known it and to turn from the holy commandment delivered to them. But it has happened to them according to the true proverb..."*[21]

Let's talk about a covenant relationship between a father and a son for a moment. Being a father to so many sons all over the world, I will tell you that fatherhood is much like playing poker. You never give all five cards to your son. *Remember, the most precious and valuable card is the one that the son doesn't get until the father dies.*

Look at the Biblical prophet Elijah and his spiritual son, Elisha. Elisha pressed so hard at the end of Elijah's life, because he "wanted it so bad." But Elijah's (paraphrased) response was, *"I* can't decide to give it to you. Now you can be a look-a-like if you want, but if you're real, you'll stick it out to the end, and *God* will give it to you."

A word that is sometimes used interchangeably with the word "covenant" is the word "testament." In examining the way that a testament, or a will, is executed, we can see that there are some vital and valuable aspects of a covenant relationship that do not exchange hands until death. In the book of Hebrews, the writer tells us, *"Now when someone dies and leaves a will, no one gets anything until it is proved that the person who wrote the will is dead. The will goes into effect only after the death of the person who wrote it. While the person is still alive, no one can use the will to get any of the things promised to them."*[22]

The requirements of any "testament" are as follows:

+ The Testator
+ The Heirs
+ The Goods
+ The Testator's Death
+ The Fact of the Death Brought Forward

21. 2 Peter 2:21-22
22. Hebrews 9:16-17, *NLT*

+ The Witnesses

+ The Seal

Once again, that fifth card never comes out until the father dies. This is the final test. Will you stick it out to the very end, to get your *full inheritance*?

When you have four cards, you may look just like the original, but you're not the original. The original is the one that says, *"Where is the Lord God of Elijah?"* He doesn't say, "Now, I want to leave and do *my own thing*. Now, I want to have *my own name.*" Elisha's requirement, in order to receive a double portion of Elijah's anointing, was to stick with Elijah until the very end. Covenant means you make a vow *to never leave.* It means you are willing to stay, long after others have said good-bye. Only then do you get the prize.

King Solomon observed, *"There is a friend who sticks closer than a brother... A true friend was born for the days of real difficulty."*[23] A friend is the only one who is willing to stay, long after everyone else has said good-bye. A friend will not pick up and go. He will stick close to you, and

> COMMITMENT IS THE WILLINGNESS TO STAY, LONG AFTER OTHERS HAVE SAID GOOD-BYE.

consistently give you sweet counsel. Says Proverbs, *"The heartfelt counsel of a friend is sweet; it's as sweet as perfume and incense. **Never abandon a friend...**"*[24] *If you faint in the day of adversity, your strength is small."*[25] It is in the day of adversity that a person will find out who his true friends are. True covenant friendships stay. They are in your life for the long haul.

The Law of Covenant is critical to any meaningful relationship. Covenant relationship is a sacred gift that is vital for your protection, promotion, pursuit of truth, character building, and longevity. Value it highly for the precious treasure that it is.

---

23. Proverbs 18:24; 17:17, author's paraphrase
24. Proverbs 27:9-10 *NLT*, author's paraphrase
25. Proverbs 24:10

THE LAW OF COVENANT

The mark of a healthy relationship is security,
which is a result of trust.

→ To seek the benefits (promises) of a covenant relationship without meeting the conditions is considered a breach of the covenant.

→ The most accurate test of character occurs when we are thrown into the lion's den of humanity.

→ Character ensures the integrity of covenant.

→ The prodigal feels that he is *entitled* to the resources of another, while the protégé responds to whatever he receives with heartfelt gratitude.

→ Your value in any relationship is determined by your diversity.

→ Your value in any relationship is the *difference* that you can bring, to cause success to come to your friend.

→ Your value to others is in direct proportion to the problems you solve for them.

→ A covenant not made is a covenant not enjoyed.

→ The evidence of love is the pledge to protect.

→ The only difference between control and correction lies in the heart of the receiver.

→ The manner in which you treat a relationship when you no longer need it reveals the motive you had for it from the beginning.

→ Commitment is the willingness to stay, long after others have said good-bye.

THE LAW OF
SINGLE
PURPOSE

The celebration of any relationship
is dependent upon the clear definition
of purpose and vision.

4

THE CELEBRATION OF ANY RELATIONSHIP IS DEPENDENT UPON THE CLEAR DEFINITION OF PURPOSE AND VISION.

A crucial factor in covenant relationship is the singleness of purpose. In a world where diversification and tolerance are concepts that are almost worshiped, the necessity for unification and singleness of purpose has nearly been lost.

WRITE THE VISION

When God gave a prophet of old an assignment, He instructed him, *"Write the vision, and make it plain…that whoever reads it will take it up and run with it!"*[1] The prophet was told to *write it*, not only to clearly imprint it upon his own mind and heart, but especially to lay down a roadmap for others. God desired that the purpose of His heart would reach those in distant places, would excite and

---
1. Habakkuk 2:2, author's paraphrase

motivate those in future ages, and would not fall into oblivion. What is handed down by tradition and word of mouth is easily altered and liable to corruption; but *what is written* is reduced to a certainty, and is preserved safe and pure.

The prophet was told to write the vision *and make it plain.* Obviously, God thought it was extremely important that His vision, plan, and purpose be preserved and accurately communicated to faithful men, who would carry it out with focus and excellence. He knew that the vision would affect not only those living in the present, but also countless generations to come.

It is for these same reasons that we must be very selective in whom we are in covenant with, as we work to carry out the vision that God has assigned to us. If we attempt to build relationships with people who seem to constantly question or thwart our efforts to "run with the vision," God's Divine plan for our lives will be divided, diluted, and finally come to nothing.

> SATAN CANNOT ARRANGE YOUR DEMISE; BUT HE IS THE AUTHOR OF CONFUSION.

Satan cannot arrange your demise; but he is the author of confusion. If you are embracing Godly principles in your life, then you are a winner, walking in supernatural favor and protection, and Satan knows it. Therefore, unless you leave an 'open door,' through doubt, ignorance, or unbelief, he cannot schedule destruction that would ruin you or cause you to come to nothing. His only hope is to send distractions to divide the focus of your life. He knows that if you succumb to distraction, your dream, your vision, and your life will ultimately be destroyed.

The devil's most effective form of distraction is poor relationships. He will actually twist and distort the holy concepts of mercy and love, in order to get you to commit yourself to someone whom he has sent to distract, divide, and destroy you!

Di-vision is simply *two visions.* If the enemy can lure you into building a relationship with someone who can *divide your focus* and your energies, then he has effectively stopped you from fulfilling Heaven's plan for your life. And remember, if this happens, it will not be you alone who will suffer. Generations to come will be robbed of what God intended for them to have, and the plans and purposes of God will be hindered and impeded.

> **DI-VISION IS SIMPLY TWO VISIONS.**

Therefore, it is of the utmost importance that *singleness of purpose* be a factor, when you are looking to qualify your relationships. You must actively search for those who are *one with you* in heart, mind, and purpose. Whether you realize it or not, when God gives someone a vision, He has also assigned specific people to help that individual carry out that vision. It has already been recorded in their book of days,[2] that they were created and equipped to be a part of that specific team, and that specific purpose.

You may be the man or woman with the vision—you must find those who have been assigned to you. Or, you may be a soldier in the army of the faithful, ready to serve and contribute your unique talents and gifts—you must find the one to whom you've been assigned. We must each find our place. We must each embrace our God-ordained assignment. And then, my friend, we must *run with it!*

IN ONE ACCORD

The Apostle Paul encouraged his friends that only when they "*...with one mind and one mouth glorify God...*"[3] would they see measurable success in their lives. The Greek word used in this context is translated "*with one accord.*" It means to act in unity, with one purpose, without contentions, clashes, or strife.[4] Paul is exhorting these people to think the same thoughts, to be of the same viewpoints and decisions, and because of their love for God, to yoke themselves together in harmonious unity and like-mindedness in every facet of life.

Notice that Paul uses the phrase "one mind and one mouth." It is not sufficient that there be one mouth, but there must also be one mind, for God looks at the

2. See Psalms 139:16
3. Romans 15:6
4. *Barnes' Notes*, Electronic Database. Copyright (c) 1997 by Biblesoft.

heart. In fact, there cannot consistently be one mouth where there is not one mind, and God's purposes can only be realized where there is a fusion of both.

Paul later writes to his family in Philippi, saying, *"...make me truly happy by agreeing wholeheartedly with each other, loving one another, and working together with one heart and purpose."*[5] The Greek word for *"be of one mind"* means *to think the same thing, in unity of heart, of feeling, of opinion, of plan, and of purpose; to move together as if only one soul was activating you.*[6] He wished them to avoid all division and strife, being united in one common cause.

BUILT ON TRUTH AND LOVE

The foundation of all covenant relationship and excellent endeavor is laid in like-mindedness, partnership in integrity, and an agreement to love. Like-mindedness is the *willingness to mind the same thing,* to remove all grounds for differences, and to lay all quarrels aside.

We begin to approach like-mindedness when we have the same love. We should be one in affection, whether or not we can be one in vision. Having the same love is always in our power, always our duty, and is the likeliest way to bring us nearer to unity of mind and purpose. Being of one accord and of one mind implies not crossing and thwarting aspirations, or pursuing separate interests.

This like-mindedness must be according to truth, however. *Truth, not error, must be at the core of our unity.* It is a counterfeit harmony if we are binding together to give our power and strength to what is wrong. This would be like-mindedness resembling the Babel-builders, who were united in their rebellion.[7] We must strive *first for truth,* and then for peace; for this is the wisdom that is from above—it is first pure, then peaceable.[8]

> TRUTH, NOT ERROR, MUST BE AT THE CORE OF OUR UNITY.

---

5. Philippians 2:2, *NLT*
6. *Barnes' Notes,* Electronic Database. Copyright (c) 1997 by Biblesoft.
7. See Genesis 11:6
8. See James 3:17

The Law of Single Purpose infers that we are perfectly agreed in laboring together, to promote the plans and purposes of One greater than ourselves. Being of one mind, we are focused and intent upon this grand vision, keeping our eyes fixed upon it in all we say, do, or intend.

GREAT VISIONS REQUIRE GREAT TEAMS

Attempting to accomplish your vision alone will guarantee that your endeavor will be limited in size and effectiveness. Large visions require many supporters and unified teamwork. There is immense power and creative energy within the intricate knitting together of like-minded yet diverse relationships.

Unity does not mean eliminating diversification. On the contrary, the greater the diversification, the more effective is the team. Unity simply means that all these diversified talents are agreed and focused on achieving *the same goal.* They have iden-

> IMAGINATION IS THE
> DISCOVERY OF OPTIONS.
> FOCUS IS THE REMOVAL
> OF OPTIONS.

tified their single most important mission, and are now jointly rallying around it. Their shared passion and mission is so important that it causes irritations to be overlooked, disputes to dissolve, and formerly alienated individuals to yoke together and commit to the common cause. When this kind of unity is achieved, the impossible quickly becomes not only possible, but probable!

Although creative differences in tastes, talents, approaches to problem solving, and so on, are to be celebrated and used to their greatest advantage, there must be focused and fundamental agreement on certain key issues, if one is ever going to accomplish a goal. What are some of these important issues?

OUR FUTURE DESTINATION

To make wise decisions and see everyone's goals accomplished, you must begin to think long-term. Immediately, in the beginning of every relationship, you must look long-term and ask yourself some very critical questions:

* What are the mutual benefits of this relationship?
* Where could this relationship take me?
* What are the possibilities?
* Are we like-minded?
* Are we moving in the same direction?
* Do we speak the same 'language'?
* Do we have the same long-term goals?
* What are the things that God can do through this relationship?
* What goals could be accomplished through this relationship that would be virtually impossible without it?
* What changes would God make in my life, if I began to invest in this relationship right now?
* How will this relationship affect my future?
* How can I add value to this new relationship?

One of the things that we must remember is that we are people who can actually *choose* our destiny. God has given us the opportunity to choose our future; and a crucial element in choosing our future is choosing the correct relationships. Friend, whether we realize this or not, the decisions that we make concerning our relationships today, will determine the outcome of our lives tomorrow.

We must seek to build our lives not only with those who have a common vision, but also with those who can take us further than we could ever go on our own. Anytime that you embrace people who cannot take you further than you are, you are proving to yourself that you are in a downward spiral.

You must understand your flesh. Your flesh is deceitful. The ancient prophet

Jeremiah said, *"The heart is deceitful above all things and desperately wicked. Who can know it?"*[9] You simply cannot know your own heart. The only way you can know where you are is by taking a look at your life. The truth is revealed in the study hall of life, where you stop listening to yourself and you begin to watch yourself. This is the only way you can truly tell where you are. You must ask yourself some very fundamental questions:

* What are the unpleasant things that I am tolerating in my life right now?
* What are things that I would never allow in the past, but I now seem to be embracing?
* What are the things that used to repulse me, but now I'm letting them happen?
* What are the things that I would never let my eyes see before, but now they seem almost commonplace?

Consider this scenario: You know that there are negative individuals around you—you may have gossipers around you, or people who don't have strong moral standards. Those individuals *are* affecting you and taking you down the path of compromise, even if you insist, "They're not, they're not; they're not influencing me!" You cannot avoid the fact that *the snapshot of your future is taken with the people of your present.*

> THE SNAPSHOT OF YOUR FUTURE IS TAKEN WITH THE PEOPLE OF YOUR PRESENT.

Soon, you will find yourself somewhere in life that you swore you would never go—because those whom you allow to surround you and affect your thought pattern are the people who will determine the outcome of your life. This is unavoidable, regardless of your present belief system.

9. Jeremiah 17:9

OUR COMMON PURPOSE

Another issue that must be agreed upon, if I am to build a relationship with someone, is *common purpose*. Purpose defines everything I do with my life—why I get up in the morning, how I choose to invest my time, and where I choose to sow my seed. My daily agenda and my twenty-five year goals are all driven by the *purpose* of my life. That purpose is found in Proverbs 22:29—

DO YOU SEE A MAN WHO EXCELS IN HIS WORK?
HE WILL STAND BEFORE KINGS; HE WILL NOT STAND BEFORE UNKNOWN MEN.

I am determined to excel in my work. Excellence—that is my passion! How could I possibly sustain a relationship with someone whose purpose was not in accordance with God's purpose for my life? Why would I even want to? How can two walk together unless they agree upon this most fundamental issue?

You must consider the plans and purposes of God to be the most serious matter in your life. *Never* give your precious, holy vision to superficial, uncommitted people of questionable character. These things are far too valuable to be put in the hands of someone who will resist, disrespect, and dishonor the direction of your life. If certain people are consistently disputing or defying you, it is time to turn your attention and affection elsewhere. It is *their* recalcitrant reactions to you that have now determined that you cannot afford to be in relationship with them. The treasure of your dream is far too costly to be deposited into ungrateful consumers. You must nurture relationship with *contributors, not consumers.*

My relationships must be confined to those whose loyalty and allegiance are towards the same directions and purposes that compel me. They must be very selective, and include only those who feel a connection, a commitment, and a sense of obligation to the same vision. Otherwise, the outcome of these relationships will only cause *di-vision* in my life

In life, there remains little left to be said, but much to be done. Have you noticed that you really don't have to say very much to the like-minded people who are around your life? Much is understood already, because our hearts are knit together by the same direction and purposes. I don't have to say anything; they know. I can say "ditto," and ditto would be the truth. It doesn't become a test of wills any longer,

> IN LIFE,
> THERE REMAINS LITTLE
> LEFT TO BE SAID
> BUT MUCH TO BE DONE.

because I have chosen to surround myself with those who are willing to focus the bulk of their time, energy, finances, and talent into *eternal priorities* rather than *temporal pleasures.*

Eternal goals and visions are the only ones that will last. It is emptiness and futility to pour your life into dreams and purposes that will produce only temporal results. Your greatest investment of attention and devotion must be directed toward spiritual and eternal matters. This eternal focus then becomes the distinctive qualifier for every relationship.

OUR ALLIED PLAN OF ATTACK

In flipping through the channels, late one night, I came across the old classic Charlton Heston movie, "Ben Hur." The scene was showing him and his fellow criminal/slaves, chained together in the belly of a battleship, painfully pulling the oars in synchronization, in an attempt to move and maneuver the huge vessel in such a way that the battle could be won. As I watched, I noticed the plight of these men—they were all chained together to the same bench, pulling on the same oar, working at the same speed and rhythm to achieve the same purpose. When one of them collapsed from sheer exhaustion, his load had to be pulled by the others, or else they *all* got whipped and punished. Their very lives depended on their ability to pull together, work as a team, and have an allied plan of attack.

As I watched this scene, I thought to myself how well it illustrated the crucial importance of this Law of Single Purpose. We, too, are in a battle of monumental proportions, and we must chain ourselves to the oars with like-minded brothers and sisters who will think the same, speak the same, move the same, work the same, and breathe the same vision and purpose. If even one of us stops rowing, consequences will come to all of us. How absolutely critical it is that we use supernatural discernment in deciding who will be chained to the oar with us!

I must bind myself only with faithful, proven, committed soldiers, with whom I am united in purpose to stand strong, to face our enemy head-on, and to fight courageously. I must never entrust my focus or my seed to someone with whom I could not trust my life; because essentially, they are one and the same.

REMAINING UNIFIED

Remaining like-minded and unified in purpose while under enemy attack is not an easy thing to do. All good soldiers have spent countless grueling hours disciplining themselves to move and react not as individuals, but *as one single unit.* Only when this unity is maintained can there ever be a hope of winning the battle.

I have found that excellent soldiers retain specific traits that give them a propensity for unity. These traits become invaluable assets in the day of battle, when single vision and unity of purpose become matters of life and death. Let's take a look at some of these assets.

The Ability to Submit

> SUBMISSION REMAINS LIFELESS UNTIL AGREEMENT BREATHES ITS FINAL SIGH.

True commitment and unity are never tested in times of agreement. Only when conflict and dissension arise, can one's commitment to unity be exposed. Why is this true? Because *submission remains lifeless until agreement breathes its final sigh.*

This test will come to *every* mentor/protégé relationship, whether it's officer/soldier, parent/child, boss/employee, teacher/student, or pastor/church member. A wise person understands that when he submits to his authority, he is submitting *to God, through that person*. **Submission is simply the willingness to bow my knee before men, in order to satisfy the requirements of heaven.**

Plainly put, submission is no more than victory over self-will. A person with a submitted heart will be more interested in what his leader wants than in what *he* wants. He knows that <u>sub</u>-mission means, "I put my mission below our collective mission." My response must always be, "The answer is yes—now what is the question?" The only time a submitted individual would even think of jumping out in front of his leader, would be to protect and shield him from the malicious attacks of his enemies.

> SUBMISSION
> IS THE WILLINGNESS
> TO BOW MY KNEE
> BEFORE MEN, IN ORDER
> TO SATISFY THE
> REQUIREMENTS OF HEAVEN.

Passing the test of submission is the first step in being part of an effective team, and it is an absolute requirement in discerning if someone is truly like-minded and assigned to your future.

The Ability to Serve

Servanthood has nothing to do with menial tasks done by an unskilled, low-positioned workforce. Servanthood is about character and attitude. You can easily sense when someone acts "put out" at the prospect of helping others. You can also sense when someone has a heart to serve—their focus is on others, not on themselves.

An insecure, fearful person finds it very difficult to become a true servant, because he is too busy protecting himself. His insecurity is often communicated as pride, self-importance, or snobbery; but beneath that edgy exterior is a heart of extremely low self-esteem and bankrupt self-confidence. It is impossible for a person to hide his self-image. It is always revealed in how he treats others. If he disrespects others, it is because he does not respect himself. If he is critical and condemning of others, it is because he feels guilty and condemned. And if he feels loved, encouraged, and valuable, he will be able to love, empower, validate, and serve others.

A like-minded servant has one thing in his sights, and that is providing whatever help is necessary to see his leader's Divinely imparted goals and objectives fulfilled. He is not simply putting his own schedule on hold just long enough to fulfill his leader's requests (although many people cannot even bring themselves to do this!) Rather, he is purposefully focusing his attention and awareness on his authority's needs, without question. He exhibits an approachable attitude, an attitude of being available and willing to assist him, and to consider his needs and feelings as valuable. He responds to directives with unhesitating submission and unquestioning obedience. He stays alert and sensitive to each and every nuance expressed by his leader, whether it comes in the form of a request or a preference. He pays attention to detail and anticipates any needs that may unexpectedly arise. Eventually, the true servant will not need to be told what to do, for he will know his mentor's heart as he knows his own.

A servant's heart will compel him to be *genuinely interested* in his mentor's vision. This is not a feigned interest in order to position himself to *receive*, but rather an alert, attentive interest in order to position himself *to sow his greatest asset…HIS LIFE.* A servant's motive is not to seek an opportunity to arrogantly parade his talents and abilities, but to selflessly share his gifts to bless and benefit others. He is not consumed with thoughts of exalting his own reputation, or receiving the praise, recognition, and honor of *men.* If he is to receive any honor or recognition, he wants it to come *from God,* first and foremost. But it is one of the paradoxical ironies of God's kingdom, that this type of selfless servant *will,* inevitably, get recognized and promoted! Anyone who is willing to serve at the lowest level *will* eventually flourish at the highest.

The Ability to Support

A good way to look at the issue of supporting someone is to imagine the work of a support beam, in a huge building. What would be some of the adjectives you might use in describing its role and function?

* Solid
* Enduring
* Rooted
* Stable
* Constant
* Grounded
* Not easily shaken, moved or affected by outside forces

Now let's personalize the use of these adjectives. A *person* who is supportive will demonstrate the following character traits, both in attitude and in action:

* Steadfast
* Reliable
* Predictable
* Responsible
* Unbending in character and purpose
* Immovable in matters of principle
* Dependable enough to be counted on
* Strong enough to be leaned on
* Steady enough to hold things together, even when circumstances seem to shake the foundations of life.

Diligence is also a requirement for those who truly desire to support a person and his dreams. The writer of Hebrews said, *"...He [God] is a rewarder of those who diligently seek Him."*[10] The Greek word for "diligently" is *ekzeteo*, and it presents the picture of *one who seeks something so passionately and determinedly that he literally exhausts all his power in his search; someone who is hardworking, attentive, busy, constant, and persistent in one's devotion to what he or she is doing.*[11]

A supportive person is *willing* to do whatever it takes to get a job done. He disciplines himself to do what he ought to do, before granting himself the pleasure of doing what he would like to do. He lives to see his leader's goals promoted and advanced, knowing that what he makes happen for his leader, God will make happen for him. Providing strength, assistance, and courage to his leader, and seeing his leader's God-given vision come to pass are his primary objectives and

---

10. Hebrews 11:6
11. Rick Renner, *Sparkling Gems from the Greek* (Tulsa, OK: Teach All Nations, 2003), p. 102.

motivations. This attitude of sacrificial willingness and obedience contributes immensely to the unity of any team.

The Ability to Communicate

Very few things are as crucial to the unity of mind and purpose as is communication. Unity and like-mindedness are built on trust, and the only way to establish trust is through honest, thorough, and open communication.

These channels of communication must be kept constantly open, so that the *essence* of the God-given purpose is continually made clear to all. It is disheartening to attempt to perform the grueling, day-to-day duties of service, if you are not keeping the finish line in mind. We must constantly remind each other *why* we are doing what we are doing. We must exhort and encourage each other of the *eternal benefits* that will come from our temporal assignments.

There is not a sports team on the planet that could ever win a game without communication. There is no army on earth that could even hope to win a war without good communication. Surely, there is no dream or vision that can come to pass without the unity of mind, heart, and spirit that comes from that vision being enthusiastically communicated.

The Ability to Understand

Real communication has not even occurred until each party feels he has been understood. A good communicator will *seek to understand* more than he will *seek to be understood*. He realizes that the ability to understand people is the ability to influence, motivate, and unify people.

An understanding person will focus on how things are for others, rather than on how things are for himself. He knows that people respond and reach their highest potential in any situation where they feel listened to, understood, and valued. He understands that to validate someone is not necessarily to give approval to what the person is saying, but rather to acknowledge, through positive attention, a person's right to be respected and heard.

If the simple act of understanding can bring so many benefits, why are so many lives being destroyed by misunderstandings?

The following factors are barriers to being an understanding person:[12]

* Selfishness—We must put *other's* interests ahead of our own[13]
* Pre-judging a situation based on faulty information and/or fear
* Refusal to celebrate another's unique differences
* Failure to recognize how the other person is just like yourself

In protégé/mentor relationships, however, understanding a mentor is not always possible at the beginning of the relationship. If the protégé understood everything that the mentor understands, then there would be no need for the relationship! This is the stage in relationship where the protégé must *submit and trust* his mentor, even if he does not understand. This process is beneficial to the protégé, for if he is ever to become an excellent leader, he must first be a faithful and unquestioning follower. As he submits his will, and follows the direction of his mentor/teacher, his prayer to God should be, "Lord, increase my understanding!" God will honor his obedience and his prayer, and soon he will not only understand that person's heart and vision, but it will, in fact, become his own.

Unity and like-mindedness will be elusive and fleeting if understanding is disregarded. The very essence of walking together in singleness of purpose is the relief and reassurance that the other person **truly** *understands*.

The Ability to Encourage

There is nothing like having an encourager on your team. An encourager is one who *pours courage into* a person or a situation. In a world rampant with fear, an encourager is a welcome sight indeed!

People are drawn to one who encourages, just as a moth is drawn to light. To have someone believe in you and support you is extremely rare in today's climate. An encourager believes the best about people and is ready to actively invest that faith into them. His encouragement and support are not superficial flattery or patronization, but a real and sincere expression of his belief in others. He knows that it's not *problems* that defeat people—it's what people *believe* about their problems that defeats them. Remember, it is not what is done to you that determines the outcome

---

12. John C. Maxwell, *Relationships 101-What Every Leader Need To Know* (Nashville, TN: Thomas Nelson Publishers, 2003), p. 9-11.
13. See Philippians 2:2-4

of your life; it is how you respond to injustice that determines your destiny.

The goal of an encourager is *not* to get others to believe in *him*, but to get others to believe in *themselves*. As an encourager, the degree of success that you can draw out of a person will be directly proportional to the confidence you express in his ability to succeed; in other words, you get what you expect!

IT IS NOT WHAT IS DONE TO YOU THAT DETERMINES THE OUTCOME OF YOUR LIFE; IT IS HOW YOU RESPOND TO INJUSTICE THAT DETERMINES YOUR DESTINY.

If you are an encourager, you know how to speak to the king in a man, or the queen in a woman. By this I mean that there is a person of royalty and greatness inside every human being—even if presently asleep. Your confidence in an individual creates the environment that causes that royalty and greatness to awaken and rise to action.

It is the person of *influence* that holds the true seat of power. Often, this person is *not* the leader or authority figure, but someone who stays "behind the scene." Because he is willing to encourage others and focus on their strengths and abilities, he is a powerful influencer. The verbal affirmation he gives is especially effective if done in the presence of "important others" in the recipient's life (friends, family, co-workers, authority figures).

When people decide to step out and take the risks needed to pursue their dream, they may fail in the beginning; anyone who takes risks will at some point experience failure. It is then that a crucial decision must be made—will they quit or keep going? Your expressing your confidence in them may be just the nudge they need to convince them to keep going.

Tell them about *your* failures, and how responding correctly to those traumas actually equipped you for success in the future. Urge them to *never give up*. Remind them that faith boldly declares its dreams for the future, while fear finds its power from the past.

If you are an encourager, you will paint a picture of success with your words.

Your encouragement will write the vision on their hearts, so they can run with it. Without that vision, people perish.

> FAITH BOLDLY DECLARES ITS DREAMS FOR THE FUTURE, WHILE FEAR FINDS ITS POWER FROM THE PAST.

A man with a big vision must dare to believe that there is something inside of him that can transcend and conquer any circumstance. A like-minded encourager is an indispensable asset in continually reaffirming such a belief, and uniting the whole team around that goal.

The Ability to Bear Pain

Unity within a large group of people is not possible unless each individual is willing and able to repeatedly say "NO!" to his own needs, desires, opinions, and preferences. Saying "no" to oneself and "yes" to the vision, over and over again, is not an easy task—it can be painful, frustrating, and draining, both emotionally and physically.

A person who has tied himself, heart and soul, to another's dream is willing and able to bear the pressure and pain of helping to carry that vision to its completion. He is willing to sacrifice his own comfort and well being for the advancement of the covenant relationship that he has entered.

Knowing that true friends have the same enemies, a like-minded partner will do the painful work of ending previous relationships, if that is what must be done to pursue an undivided and focused future. He will endure the pain of scorn and rejection, in order to preserve his commitment to the covenant and the vision.

Nothing of any value comes easily, or without pain. Dreams and visions are birthed from the pain of discipline, self-correction, public ridicule, and the elimination of options, even when those options are good and beneficial, in and of themselves.

The Ability to Change

A person who pursues a big future must also embrace flexibility and change. Show me something that never grows or changes, and I'll show you something

that is dead. A God-given vision is a living entity, an ever blooming and blossom-
ing seed that increases and multiplies to the degree that we pursue its fulfillment.

A person who runs with the vision is a problem-solver. The words, "I can't"
are not a part of his vocabulary, because he doesn't accept that there is anything
that is impossible to him. He believes that when he becomes a problem solver, he
can solve any problem that he has, or any problem that is brought to him. He is
flexible and ready to act upon the solution when he receives it.

A leader's attainment of his goal is largely determined by the attitudes of those
who are following him. For instance, the success of my life is greatly dependent
upon Linda's attitude. If she digs her heels in the sand and refuses to grow or to
become what God wants her to become, I'm finished. She may end up being what
she wants to be, but *I'm* the one that is stopped. At that point, I have one of two
choices: I can compromise my integrity and my commitment to Divine principles,
or I can say, "Linda, I'm sorry, you must become what God has called you to
become, and there are no two ways about it." That's why, when partners begin to
move and change and grow, they must move *in unison*.

Whether you are a partner in marriage or a partner in another covenant relationship, these traits are valuable tools in preserving the unity of heart, mind, and
spirit that is vital to the health of any relationship and the fulfillment of any vision.

DISCERNING YOUR BRETHREN

It is not always easy to find like-minded people, but it is well worth the search.
You will produce more with one like-minded person of average talent, than you ever
could with one hundred greatly talented people who want to do things *their way*.

In searching for those who can pass the test of Single Purpose in your life, you
must remember not to listen with your ears; always 'listen' with your eyes. Your eyes
will tell you more than your ears ever will. Watch! Do you want to find out what a

person's value system is? *Watch what they do.* Don't just read a person's resume—"I can do this and this and this…" No! The Apostle Paul was smarter than that. He said, "*I do not want you to think of me above that which you **see me do…**"*[14]

In identifying those who have been assigned to you, always keep in mind the central objective of *being of one mind.*[15] The Greek word for this phrase is *homophron,* which is translated *"of the same mind."*[16] It is speaking about two people who have the same thoughts, reason things out the same way, and reach the same conclusions. They have the same viewpoints, understandings, and feelings about the issues of life. Therefore, they can *effectively* work together toward the same goal, purpose, and vision. Their unity of heart and vision brings world-transforming power to their relationship, their organization, and their endeavor.

Finding these kinds of relationships does not usually happen by coincidence; like-minded people do not just 'happen' to find each other. *Investment* is required for two people to attain like-mindedness. It takes focus, concentration, and deliberate decision on their part. Unity does *not* mean the elimination or resolution of all disagreements. It means that people have a deep desire to see the future the same way, and are willing *to work* on being *in one accord* in purpose, strategy, and passion. They have chosen to be compassionate toward one another, for *compassion* is the process of being united and cemented together in passion, feeling, and emotion; it is making the choice to embrace and experience *with* someone whatever he is passionate about. These are the kinds of people you are looking to build your life with.

The biblical term for someone who is united with you to this degree is "brethren." More than simply a "brother" who understands your personal challenges and triumphs in life, "brethren" implies a fellow soldier in the fight, someone who will 'watch your back' and never desert you, even in the heat of intense enemy fire. Your brethren are your comrades in battle, those who are still with you on the frontlines when so many others have given up the fight and left. "Brethren" implies that you've been through so much together that words can no longer communicate the depth and intensity of your common bond of experi-

---

14. 2 Corinthians 12:6, author's paraphrase
15. See 1 Peter 3:8
16. James Strong, *The New Strong's Exhaustive Concordance of the Bible* (Nashville, TN: Thomas Nelson Publishers, 1990) p. 783/52.

ence; but that's OK, because that bond is experienced at such a gut level that words are no longer necessary. Your brethren are those whom you can trust implicitly and can count on to stay faithful to the cause.[17]

DEALING WITH BETRAYAL

Have you ever entered a significant relationship with someone whom you believed was like-minded and committed to the same vision, only to have this person stab you in the back and betray you? I doubt that there is a mentor or leader anywhere who has escaped such heartbreak.

When this kind of treachery rips into your life, it's very tempting to pull back, nurse your wounds, and get very cynical about ever trusting anyone again. But trust you must! First, you must trust that God will heal your broken heart and help you to forgive, so that you can be free from bitterness. Then, you must trust Him to show you the *faithful brethren* surrounding you—those who are worthy of your trust and your impartation into their lives. There *are* individuals who have the same heart, the same goal, and the same vision as you; the key is to accurately identify them.

Any devastating experience can become an incredible learning experience, if you can lay your emotions aside and examine it with eyes of objectivity. My dear friend and co-laborer in ministry, Rick Renner, has used the following questions in attempting to gain insight into situations of personal betrayal:[18]

* Did I give too much authority to this person too quickly?
* Did I trust someone I really didn't know very well?
* Did I spend enough time with that person to really become his friend?
* Did I let that person know what I expected of him?
* Did I ignore signs that something was going amiss?

---

17. Rick Renner, *Sparkling Gems from the Greek* (Tulsa, OK: Teach All Nations, 2003), p. 35-36.
18. Ibid, p. 550.

* Did my spouse tell me something was wrong, but I wouldn't listen?

* What did I learn from this experience?

Friend, you must learn to identify the people who are truly your *brethren*, those who will whole-heartedly and without reservation share your heart and lock in to your vision. There are tests of integrity that must be passed before enlisting someone to be a part of your team.

Remember, the most vital element, when considering the Law of Single Purpose, is not a person's talent, abilities, or slick presentation, but rather a person's character, like-mindedness, and faithfulness. It is not commonality of culture, race, language, or religion that will bring true unity and effectiveness in impacting this world; it is becoming cemented together by a common purpose and a shared goal—it is the Law of Single Purpose.

THE LAW OF SINGLE PURPOSE

The celebration of any relationship
is dependent upon the clear definition of purpose and vision.

→ Satan cannot arrange your demise; but he is the author of confusion.

→ Di-vision is simply two visions.

→ Truth, not error, must be at the core of our unity.

→ Imagination is the discovery of options. Focus is the removal of options.

→ The snapshot of your future is taken with the people of your present.

→ In life, there remains little left to be said, but much to be done.

→ Submission remains lifeless until agreement breathes its final sigh.

→ Submission is the willingness to bow my knee before men, in order to satisfy the requirements of heaven.

→ It is not what is done to you that determines the outcome of your life; it is how you respond to injustice that determines your destiny.

→ Faith boldly declares its dreams for the future, while fear finds its power from the past.

THE LAW OF
EXCLUSIVITY

Authentic commitment demands selectivity,
not inclusivity.

5

AUTHENTIC COMMITMENT

DEMANDS SELECTIVITY, NOT INCLUSIVITY.

Pursuing like-minded people who share your purpose and vision will auto-matically narrow your field of favorable relationships. This focusing process is necessary and beneficial if you desire to keep distraction at a distance. But, the most excellent relationships in your life will come as a result of narrowing that field even further. Your most fruitful and fulfilling relationships will manifest as you apply the Law of Exclusivity.

The Law of Exclusivity tells us that the most fulfilling relationships are never inclusive. This is simply the concept of focus applied to the arena of relationships. Let me share this powerful principle with you once again: *Inspiration is the discovery of options, while focus is the elimination of them.*

When you operate in the Law of Exclusivity, you are eliminating the danger

> INSPIRATION
> IS THE DISCOVERY OF
> OPTIONS, WHILE FOCUS IS
> THE ELIMINATION OF THEM.

of building relationships with people who do not value integrity, respect, excellence, and an eternal vision. You are choosing to focus upon and pursue only those relationships that qualify to receive the most precious seed of your life —TIME!

EXCLUSIVITY OR FAVORITISM?

At first glance, exclusivity may appear to be a fancy word for favoritism, which is distasteful at best. But a closer examination reveals some crucial differences between these two concepts.

What exactly is favoritism? It is extending privileges based upon an individual's personality, status, or buying power. Exclusivity (extending favor) is dependent upon another's attitude, pursuit, and productivity in the relationship. There may always be those that you favor, but you must not show favoritism.

Favoritism rests upon the personal tastes, opinions, and preferences of an individual. The judgments made about others are very subjective and volatile, easily affected by prejudice, bias, and tainted information. Exclusivity, by contrast, rests upon the desire to honor the Divine unchanging principles of integrity and truth. These principles become the *objective* standard of measure by which all things, including relationships, are judged and evaluated.

> A DOUBLE STANDARD
> IS ONLY ACCEPTABLE
> TO A HYPOCRITE.

In honoring these principles, personal preference and opinion are forsaken; only the truth matters. Those who *embrace and do the truth* are shown *favor*. The following principle tells you how to stay free from favoritism, in your relationships: *A double standard is only acceptable to a hypocrite.*

Let it always be said of you, that you are a person of principle. Never break principle, no matter who or what comes into your life. Never be interested in choosing one person over another or in living your life by a double standard—in allowing one person to act a certain way, while punishing another for the same behavior.

PROTECTING THE "CIRCLE"

I believe that God sends people into your life to protect you. You have to make certain that you do not reject these relationships; otherwise you will become a person of mediocrity and compromise, who sabotages the safety and sanctuary that God wants to provide for you.

The children of our generation have been unprotected from the cancer of inclusive associations. In their search for a significant connection and relationship, they have intimate romantic relations with several people, and it doesn't presently bother them. They have no understanding of real love or the future consequences that now become unavoidable. Remember this: Love has loyalty within it. Love has *exclusivity* within it.

In this culture of tolerance and indulgence, exclusivity in relationship is seen as narrow-minded at best, and bigoted or criminal at worst. And yet, genuine commitment says, "I take *you*, and I forsake all others." This commitment to protect your "circle" of relationships is vital if you intend to stay focused and fulfill God's vision for your life.

Of course, I am respectful and considerate to people outside of my "circle," but I steer clear of their ability to influence me. If and when I see them or talk to them, I do it on my terms, not theirs. I can give people unconditional *acceptance* —because of the love and mercy of God; but I cannot give them unconditional *approval*—because of the righteousness and justice of God. *"How can righteousness have fellowship with unrighteousness?—For you are the temple of the living God..."*[1] Remember, any relationship that attempts to take your focus away from God, His Word, or His plan for your life, has to be set off to the side.

---

1. 2 Corinthians 6:14-16, 1 Corinthians 3: 17, author's paraphrase

CAN LIGHT AND DARKNESS CO-EXIST?

You cannot cultivate relationship with darkness, and still remain in the light! What fellowship can light have with darkness? They cannot co-exist in the natural realm; neither can they co-exist in the realm of your relationships. Don't spend an entire lifetime with the wrong person and end up getting your brains beat out in the end!

I have seen countless numbers of people fall, because they hang around with the wrong people. Whenever you come into a person's presence, the atmosphere they carry with them is either positive or negative. If you begin to feel that there is a negative ambience, you need to pull yourself from that person quickly, because you're not helping him or yourself if you stay.

Did you know that there are people that even God can't help? This was one of the hardest lessons I ever had to learn! It's a funny thing—*we* think we can correct someone that can't be corrected by God Himself. The Bible advises us *"not to keep company with anyone named a brother,* (anyone who claims to be a Christian) *who is sexually immoral or covetous, an idolater or a reviler; if a "brother" is an angry person, a drunkard or an extortioner, we are not even to eat with that person."*[2] The Apostle Paul said we are not even to have lunch with the man. You will not help them by being with them, but *they will hurt you* by being with them; *bad company corrupts good and moral behavior.*[3] Paul later went on to say, *"And if anyone does not obey our word in this epistle, note that person and do not keep company with him, that he may be ashamed."*[4]

Friend, if you keep company with people who are in rebellion, *you won't shame them into repentance; rather they will shame you into backsliding.* They will get you to a place where you will begin to doubt the truths you know.

Destruction comes because you sit around and you talk to people who don't embrace Divine principle. You see, if I want to know what's going on with you, I don't need to ask questions—I just need to study the people around you, and that

2. 1 Corinthians 5:11, author's paraphrase
3. See 1 Corinthians 15:33
4. 2 Thessalonians 3:14

will tell me all I need to know.

In a letter sent to his protégé Timothy, Paul once wrote, *"No one engaged in warfare entangles himself with the affairs of this life, that he may please him who enlisted him as a soldier."*[5] The word "entangles" comes from the Greek word *empleko*. It describes a person entangled in his lower garments, such as a runner who was winning a race until his garments became caught between his legs. It describes something that has been so tightly woven together and intertwined that it cannot break free, and is now being hindered or endangered.[6]

I believe we can apply this statement directly to the arena of relationships. A soldier must surround himself with a company of men who will keep him focused upon the battle at hand. If he allows himself the foolishness of an indiscriminate, distracting relationship, not only will he displease the one who enlisted him, but he also could get killed!

As you pursue your assignment, it is crucial that you do not allow yourself to become entangled in relationships that will distract, hinder, or endanger you. These types of relationships not only displease the One whom we serve, but they are snares that can kill the dream placed on the inside of us.

QUALIFYING FOR RELATIONSHIP

Any relationship, if it's going to be meaningful, *must be qualified for*. At any given moment, every relationship is either taking you closer to or further from God. If you have an "open door policy" in relationships, allowing just anyone to be your friend without qualifying for your friendship, you've just shown everyone how cheap it is to become your friend.

> AT ANY GIVEN MOMENT, EVERY RELATIONSHIP IS EITHER TAKING YOU CLOSER TO OR FURTHER FROM GOD.

---

5. 2 Timothy 2:4
6. Rick Renner, *Sparkling Gems from the Greek* (Tulsa, OK: Teach All Nations, 2003), p. 47-48.

There must be prerequisites in relationship. You must never fall into friend-ships like some people fall in love. Falling implies an unexpected mishap! Quit falling—*enter by choice*. This is a revolutionary idea to most. Embrace a relation-ship because you want it, and hold on to it because you want to prolong it; but don't fall into it. We must never allow relationships to form simply because of happenstance or convenience.

You may be wondering, "How will I know who fulfills the requirements?" You don't need to wonder who a person is; a person will show you who he is. *Excellence forces mediocrity to reveal itself.* The more that you set a standard in your relationships, the more you will force those who do not have that standard to reveal themselves—because mediocre people cannot maintain standards.

If you are ever going to build anything in your life, you must be consistent. The Apostle John wrote, *"Only hold fast to that which you have already attained."*[7] Do not give up any ground that you have already conquered.

Remember, it is only through relationship that you reach your fullest potential, but this must be done with the right people. The weakest relationship in my life will be the one that takes me down. Even Jesus noted, "Haven't I chosen you twelve, and now I've discovered that one of you is a devil."[8] Who was the individual that brought the final demise of the Christ? It was his weakest relationship.

You must have principles that do not change—those that are non-negotiable. Just keep in mind that society will not celebrate your principles; society will try to change them. Mediocrity says, "If we can cause him to lower his standards, then we will never have to raise ours. But, if he refuses to move or compromise, we will have to ultimately come up to his standards."

The Law of Exclusivity helps me keep the wrong people out of my life. A per-son doesn't get to be my friend just because he sits next to me in the lunchroom. We must learn to move beyond the "hanging around" stage in relationships. Every relationship must have purpose. Without purpose, people perish. Let me explain.

Millions of our young people are perishing because they have no hope, vision, or purpose for the future. Why? Because they are spending their time with

---

7. Revelation 3:11, author's paraphrase
8. See John 13:18.

people who are going nowhere, and therefore they are going nowhere themselves. Scripture tells us, *"Where there is no vision, the people are unrestrained..."*[9]

One of the best ways to keep your vision alive is to pursue others with vision. I persistently pursue great people who I desire as friends in my life. I don't care how long it takes to qualify, in their eyes. It doesn't matter to me. I am not quitting.

The level of the relationship will determine your degree of pursuit and attention. I have circles of relationships. First, I have relationships that are intimate—those I contact more than once per week. Then, there is the second circle of relationships—those that I must see or talk to once every two weeks, in order to stay connected. Lastly, I have my thirty-day relationships. But, if I am going to keep any quality relationship, I can never allow that relationship to go over thirty days without personal contact. One of the beauties of e-mail is that I am able to make contact when time affords me the ability to do so, in order to nurture that relationship and keep my name in front of that person.

I continually make myself *qualify* for friendships with the great. I continually work on my demeanor, my vocabulary, and my ability to turn on the burners when I see other people backing down. When others slow down, I'll turn on the gas. It was said of Ruth, *"We have heard about you, that you are better to your mother-in-law than seven sons."*[10] I realized that by choice, on purpose, I could become more important and significant in a person's life than even his closest relatives.

> IF YOU DESIRE
> TO BE GREAT, YOU MUST
> QUALIFY FOR ACCESS
> TO THE GREAT.

I never attempt to play a part that I haven't been given, in any relationship. I play who I am, and then I search for that place where I can become more meaningful to that person. "How can I become more meaningful to you? What requirements will it take for me to become greater in your eyes? I desire to be better to you than seven sons, or seven other friends. I will be better to you than all seven of them put together!"

---

9. Proverbs 29:18, *NAS*
10. Ruth 4:15, author's paraphrase

God desires to bring every one of you before great men and women. He has placed them in front of you, but they're not going to invite you in because you smile nice, or because you're a wonderful person! Significant people are simply too busy to negotiate this type of foolishness. They don't care if you are cool or not. They have stringent requirements for relationship.

MY QUALIFICATIONS FOR FRIENDSHIP

I had the privilege of meeting perhaps one of the greatest evangelists of our time. As soon as we were introduced, he exclaimed, "Robb, it is so good to meet you! You would not believe how many times I have heard about you. People all over the world tell me, 'You need to meet Robb Thompson. You two should be friends.'"

"Well," I said. "Sir, it would be an honor to have a friend of your caliber. Let us begin to move down that road of relationship."

We exchanged e-mail addresses and cell phone numbers, and promised to work toward a friendship.

A few days later, I e-mailed him.

"Sir," I wrote. "It was a pleasure meeting you the other day. I know you are probably very busy and would not want to waste your time or mine with niceties. I know we talked about building a friendship. I am sure you have qualifications for friendship; so do I, and here are mine."

Why did I do this? Over the last two decades of my journey, I've had many relationships—some that broke my heart, and others that restored and refreshed my soul. I would have saved myself a tremendous amount of pain and valuable time had I had requirements for relationships. There are some people who walked into my life that, quite frankly, did not belong. So, let me outline for you my six requirements for friendship, as I did for this brother in my e-mail.

1. My friends must be committed to long-lasting relationships.

My friends must be willing to live a long time in relationship with me, because I cannot bring everything that I have to offer into someone's life in just three months. I cannot add substantial value to an individual in just one year. My friends have to be willing to commit to a long lasting relationship.

Great relationships are never built short-term. There must be time for both of you to realize the investment of love and commitment. Strive to become an inheritance person, not a blessing person. Remember the Law of Covenant? Commit to stay. Yes, it is possible to benefit from a short-term relationship in the same way that a rapist can derive momentary pleasure from his inhumane act. But true friends are covenant people. They are focused on the inheritance of the relationship, not merely the blessing. They stay long after others have said good-bye. These are my friends. They are committed to long lasting relationships.

2. My friends must have empires within them.

Where are you going? What are your goals? Where do you see yourself in 10, 20, or 30 years? How do you wish to be remembered? What footprint do you want to leave in the sands of history? These are questions I ask my prospective friends. You see, *if you are going nowhere, you have already arrived.* And how can I support or stand with someone who is going nowhere? Remember, if I walk with such a person, my life also will quickly come to a halt.

My friends are busy doing exploits and producing something with their lives. They are not yet 'coming down for a landing.' They are still pressing, and they are still achieving. They will still be striving to become greater, even up to their dying breath. They just won't quit. They are world changers. They have empires in their brains.

3. My friends must be sowers.

If a person is not sowing, then he's taking. Have you ever gone to the mall or out to dinner with someone who is a taker? What a sad experience! All of a sudden, this moment we created for fellowship and love has been reduced to nothing more than to see who is going to pick up the check; and it is usually me.

Now, I realize that everyone is at different levels in their giving ability, but even in infancy, a sower is still a sower. They carry an aroma to them. They give of themselves in every situation, and always emanate a sweet fragrance of remembrance. My friends must be sowers!

4. My friends must qualify to receive my seed.

> IT IS IMPOSSIBLE FOR MY GIFT TO CHANGE THE QUALITY OF ANOTHER MAN'S HEART.

Perhaps one of the greatest lessons I have learned over the last few years is this: *It is impossible for my gift to change the quality of another man's heart.*

This is one lesson I wish I had learned earlier. Over the years, I have known many people whom I thought would change if I only showed them, through my gift, just how much I cared for them. What a huge mistake I made!

Remember the parable of the sower? In every one of those situations, it wasn't the seed or the sower that determined the return on the seed; *it was the quality of the soil* that determined the harvest.

My willingness to give you my time means I believe in you. When I sow into you, your gratitude becomes the rich soil that will produce a great harvest for our relationship. You see, every person has a harvest to yield, but few people will ever allow that harvest to be reaped from their lives. My friends must be good soil for my love, my time, and my life. Thus, they must qualify to receive my seed.

5. My friends must prize integrity above relationship.

My friends must have no doubt about what they would do if they ever had to make a choice between integrity and a relationship with me. I expect my friends to walk away from me the moment that I do not walk in virtuous character, because otherwise, I will destroy them. And I must be ready to make the same choice concerning my friends.

"But, I thought you were my friend!" Have you ever heard this statement?

Does that mean that I'm supposed to protect you while you're in the middle of doing wrong? *Not a chance;* I have to prize integrity above relationship.

Many of us are in relationships with people only because we feel sorry for them. We are in relationships with people who are needy, and we feel responsible for helping them. We are in relationships with people who want to hold on to our friendship, while at the same time, expect us to do nothing and say nothing about the wrongdoing that they are involved in. We must remember that this gives them a certain level of transferred credibility. The result is that both of us become unproductive in life.

You cannot go backwards in order to go forward, so you must prize integrity above relationship. You must take a stand for what is right and, in your integrity, get in someone's face if they are wrong over an issue. Don't let anyone compromise around you. This means that you need to be willing, even with shaking knees, to confront others over an issue. You must prize integrity above relationship.

Ponder this: *"Faithful are the wounds of a friend but the kisses of an enemy are deceitful."*[11] If a person keeps kissing up on you, watch out. Those kisses are deceiving you. Build your life with people who are courageous enough to take a stand for what is right in the face of all those who are wrong.

6. My friends must be willing to confront my enemies.

Divine precept tells me that God considers *my* enemies to be *His* enemies.[12] Likewise, my *Godly friends* consider my enemies to be their enemies. At a moment's notice and without hesitation, they will go to the mat for me against any adversary, and consider it an honor to do so.

This has been one of the most painful experiences of my Christian life—my so-called "friends" fraternizing with my enemies. We don't accept this in any other arena of life except in present day Christianity (not Biblical Christianity). We don't accept it in international diplomacy (we call them spies). We don't accept it in business (we call them unethical). We don't accept it in marriage (we call it adultery). But we do accept it in Christianity.

I am not advocating hatred or conflict, but rather, faithfulness and loyalty. You can always trust a person who will take a stand for you, and confront those who

---

11. Proverbs 27:6
12. See Exodus 14:14; 2 Chronicles 20:29; Psalm 118: 6; Psalm 124:1-2

want to destroy you. Never be afraid to stand up for a friend. If you are *neutral* today, you will be *alone* tomorrow.

Don't trust individuals who back down from confrontation when they need to confront. Putting your confidence in people like that is foolish, because you are not safe around them. The proof of love is protection.

PRESERVING HIGH STANDARDS

This life is not a dress rehearsal. We only get one shot at this, so we've got to make it count. We have no second time around on this deal. Define your standards. Set clear boundaries of right and wrong, and preserve them at all cost. Quite often, we grow so accustomed to living close to the edge that we accept too many things that have gone over it.

After his conversion, the Apostle Paul went into Damascus for 14 years. During that time, he was able to get away from some of the dangerous relationships that could have distracted him. While there, he built a strong circle of relationships with people who taught him to walk in integrity and principle.

Years later, when observing Peter's behavior in Antioch, Paul said, "Peter, I can't figure you out. When you're with the Gentiles, you act like a Gentile. But then, when the Jews come around, you reject the Gentiles and associate only with the Jews, even though you've been acting like a Gentile the whole time! Please explain to me what your standard of life is. Let's not have this shifting boundary line. What's the truth? You tell me what it is, and I can get on with you; but until you do, I am publicly rebuking you to your face, because you are to be chastised for your hypocrisy."[13] Sounds like a man who upheld truth and walked the straight and narrow.

13. See Galatians 2:11-14

REFUSE TO COMPROMISE

Compromise is the willingness to accept what you don't believe, because you are unwilling to stand for what you do. Just think of how many other things you could do in your life, if you just got rid of the compromise. This is why you must be very protective about who enters your inner circle of relationship. Exclusivity of association will keep compromise far away from you.

> COMPROMISE IS THE WILLINGNESS TO ACCEPT WHAT YOU DON'T BELIEVE, BECAUSE YOU ARE UNWILLING TO STAND FOR WHAT YOU DO.

I told my wife Linda, "Sweetheart, if it even *looks* like I'm going to try to compromise my values or faith, please get away from me. Take everything. It's all yours. I'll go out in the woods and live like the crazy man Nebuchadnezzar; he stayed there until he came to himself and realized that God was God.[14] When I find out that God is God, you can let me come home. But until that time, don't let me near you, because I would destroy your life. You have to fulfill what God has called you to do. **God has not called you to baby-sit my compromises.**"

Friend, strive to become a self-corrector. Upon close examination, your standard of excellence must become more evident, not less evident. The closer people get to you, the better you must look, because you refuse to compromise in the hidden areas of your life.

> GIANTS LEFT UNDEFEATED WILL ULTIMATELY END IN YOUR DEMISE.

A person with shifting standards encourages parasitic relationships. I like to think that I am gracious to everyone, but once I discover that an individual is a prodigal, I immediately begin to exit the relationship or restrict access. In the past, I was not as vigilant as I needed to be, and I have had to face the painful consequences of those inaccurate assessments. I have learned the hard way that *giants left undefeated will ultimately end in your demise.*

---

14. See Daniel 4:31-37

In the business world, betrayal and compromise are rampant. We have all heard about the disgruntled parasitic partner who destroys or steals the business' entire client base off the computer before he quits. Consequently, the owner must go into damage control, and may never recover from the damage caused.

Like this betrayed business partner, we have all trusted unqualified individuals. Often times, we have not been without blame. In the name of tolerance and freedom, we have **lowered the standards so that others can qualify.** You can get to a point where you talk about freedom so much that this 'freedom' becomes the very thing that conquers you and fetters you in chains.

> WHATEVER
> YOU COMPROMISE TO KEEP,
> YOU WILL
> EVENTUALLY LOSE.

Embracing compromise will destroy people both temporally and eternally. We must remember that *God* does not lower His standards so that everyone can qualify; but He does, in His mercy, provide a way so that everyone who earnestly seeks Him can *become qualified.*

Walking the straight and narrow is not always easy, fun, or popular. The price we pay, if we compromise, will often endanger the very cause we were trying to advance. Remember this principle: *Whatever you compromise to keep, you will eventually lose.*

AVOIDING DANGEROUS PEOPLE

Following this Law of Exclusivity will help you to avoid building relationships with dangerous people. Solomon emphatically stressed the importance of our associations when he said, *"He who walks with wise men shall be wise, but a companion of fools will be destroyed."*[15] You must be discriminating in your relationships. If you build relationship with wise people, you're going to become wise. But, if you hang

---

15. Proverbs 13:20

with the wrong people, your life will be destroyed. Perhaps you are wondering, "Exactly who are these dangerous people?" I have identified seven kinds of people whom you should completely avoid.

1. Those Who Feed Your Offenses

The person who feeds your offense is one of the most dangerous people you can have around you. If you follow his counsel, you will surely be damned. People who feed your rebellion are not people of your future. Watch out for these individuals, even when they are authority figures. It is damaging to keep company with an individual who undermines the respect that is due those whom God has put over me.

2. Those Who Feed Your Excess

A person who feeds your excess is an individual that will trivialize your accomplishments or blessings. They will feed the child of discontent within you. They don't encourage a spirit of gratitude in your life or in your relationships, and *you cannot experience freedom without gratitude.* Remember this: Your life cannot be stable until you make certain things

> YOU CANNOT
> EXPERIENCE FREEDOM
> WITHOUT GRATITUDE.

non-negotiable. For example, your giving must be non-negotiable. Your value system must be non-negotiable. Your faith must be non-negotiable. Your *gratitude* must be non-negotiable.

Paul wrote concerning gratitude, *"In everything give thanks, for this is the will of God..."*[16] In speaking about contentment, he said, *"...I have learned in whatever state I am, to be content."*[17]

3. Those Who Feed Your Flaws

We must avoid, at any cost, anyone who feeds our weaknesses. Are you aware that you have weaknesses in your life? I've heard people say, "You know, I went witnessing in the bar, but I ended up getting drunk—I just don't know how it happened!" I have flight attendants come to me and tell me about the Christian

---

16. I Thessalonians 5:18
17. Philippians 4:11

leaders around the world who get on airplanes and drink themselves silly, seriously tarnishing the cause of Christ. Remember this: there is somebody always watching you—*always*. Look for people who will hold you up, keep you accountable, and help you overcome your flaws.

4. Those Who Refuse to Defend You in Your Absence

One of the most difficult things that I've ever faced in my life is having people who were close to me choose not to defend me when I was not there. I couldn't

> IF I AM A TRUE FRIEND,
> I MUST NEVER FEAR OTHERS
> MORE THAN I LOVE YOU.

believe that people could live with such bad ethics. These people saw nothing wrong with failing to defend me, in order to protect their interests in another relationship.

One of the most disheartening moments anyone must endure is to be in the presence of others when someone's character is being defamed. In a recent trip to another continent, I had the privilege of meeting with some great men of God. During the conversation, these men began to dismantle another man's character.

With trembling, I replied, "You do not know the man. I know him intimately, and what you are saying is incorrect." I did this with much trembling, for all of these men were my seniors in ministry. This was one of the most difficult things I ever did.

Remember, if I am a true friend, I must never fear others more than I love you. Never continue relationship with a person who will not defend you in your absence. If you do, the day may come when you are called to walk the plank, and you'll be looking for someone to save you—but they won't be there when you need them.

5. Those Who Trivialize Your Life's Mission

Refuse to remain around someone who doesn't get excited over what is important to you. It must be important to them, if for no other reason than *it's important to you.* If it is not, then you are wasting your time with that person. If someone doesn't get excited over the mission that God has given you to fulfill in your life, you might have your plug in the wrong socket! A person who is disinterested in your dream is not interested in your future.

Some people want to know why their relationships have no meaning; *it's because they have never gotten excited over what's important to others.* The greatest way to get help in your own life is to finally get excited over what another person is excited about.

6. Those Who Feed Your Restlessness

People who incite or tolerate unfaithfulness and disobedience in your life are feeding your restlessness. Never be around a person who is a willing party to your lack of commitment. When you give your word, you *keep* your word. The futures of many people are tied up in you, and you must not let a seed of rebellion enter your heart.

Rebellion is a lingering trait in every man, woman, and child that must be continually dealt with. It is challenging enough to police your own thoughts of defiance and discontent; but fostering a relationship with a person who feeds and encourages your discontent is extremely dangerous, especially if you consider that person to be a friend.

"But Dr. Thompson," you might say. "The scripture says to *'never abandon a friend...'*"[18] All right, then we must define the term 'friend.' Remember my qualifications for friendship? Not everyone can be your friend. If someone has qualified for your friendship, indeed you should never abandon him or her. The problem is that we want to call people friends, when they are in the midst of wrongdoing. Jesus calls these types of people *sinners.* He advises us to mark and avoid them[19] and to protect the purity and exclusivity of our relationships. The Psalmist said, *"Blessed is the man who walks not in the counsel of the ungodly. Nor does he stand around with sinners.* **Nor does he sit in the seat with the disrespectful.**"[20]

7. Those Who Feed Your Uncertainties

Do you realize that the uncertainty that was introduced to the children of Israel by *only ten people* changed the future of thousands of people, for generations? Ten men who were sent to spy out the land returned and convinced all of the children of Israel that they were grasshoppers in the sight of the giants that were in the land.[21]

18. Proverbs 27:10, *NLT*
19. See Romans 16:17
20. Psalm 1:1, author's paraphrase
21. See Numbers 13-14

In the accounting of this story, the Bible says that the children of Israel cried the entire night, because those ten spies fed their uncertainty. Forty days of doubt became forty years of despair. A year for every day—one day of doubt became one year of disappointment. One day of doubt became one year of exile. One day of doubt became one year of wandering. One day of doubt became one year of losing.

Stay away from those who feed your uncertainties. The actions you take in this arena, *today*, will change you for the next forty years of your life. Changing your life isn't something that happens with your mouth alone. Changing your life is something that happens with your feet. The things you *say* need to turn into the things you *do*. When those two elements come together, your interior becomes united with your exterior. A spiritual fusion takes place, and your life changes. If you have people in your life that feed your doubts, you must rid yourself of these cancerous individuals.

WOLVES IN SHEEP'S CLOTHING

Wolves are inwardly ravenous abusers that tear up people, as well as situations. They've constantly got something negative to say and are incessantly ripping things up with their mouths.

"Those people are my friends," you might retort. "I can't just turn my back on them."

That's where you've made a mistake. You must realize that you did not turn your back on them; *they turned their back on you*. Now, you must make a choice.

> NEUTRALITY IS THE SURRENDER OF RESPONSIBILITY.

The moment you choose one person, you are rejecting another. When you choose the wolf, you are rejecting the person who has been assigned to add value to you.

THE LAW OF EXCLUSIVITY | 125

"But I just want to be neutral," you might proclaim.

This is another mistake many of us make. There is no such thing as neutrality. *Neutrality is the surrender of responsibility.* You must take either one position or the other; it is unavoidable.

"But Robb," you explain. "I don't have many friends, so I really want to work with the ones I have."

No! You have called people "friends" that have never qualified to be your friend. Dear ones, you must learn to tell the difference between a friend and a wolf. It is then that you will have the courage to apply the Law of Exclusivity to your relationships.

RELATIONSHIP LEVELS

Have you noticed that there are levels in relationships? The more invested that you become in any relationship, the more is required of you. Let me illustrate:

1. Level One

Level One relationships are fun, but shallow. These are superficial associations with friendly people who are just nice to be around. Real, significant issues don't seem to come to the foreground. However, the more invested you become at this level, the more uncomfortable the relationship may become, because new expectations of commitment are being introduced.

2. Level Two

Level Two relationships require more from you. Here, you are expected to begin to have a particular deportment; you are expected to be places on time, to keep promises, and to be more predictable. You must be much more committed and responsible, because others are counting on you. This is the level when most people choose to drop away from a relationship.

3. Level Three

The final level is what most people would refer to as 'intense and in your face.' This is when your lives become forged together. You are each willing to give up comfort, for the other. Your friend sticks closer than a brother. He is a friend, in the truest sense of the word.

Now, what happens when a Level Three relationship begins to falter? What should you do if someone is just not able to handle the demands and intensity of that level in relationship? Do you just keep the person there? No—he can't handle it. When Level Two relationships are prematurely promoted to Level Three, dishonesty will result; the person begins to put forth an effort *to appear like* he's got it together. He begins to lie—to himself and to you.

> WHAT YOU BELIEVE ABOUT A PERSON CAUSES YOU TO COME TO THEM, BUT WHAT YOU KNOW ABOUT A PERSON CAUSES YOU TO STAY WITH THEM.

We all enjoy affirming and promoting people. But if done prematurely, it becomes futile. It becomes a disservice to them and to the relationship. It is also futile to the promoter, because his growth and his vision are undermined by such a person.

NURTURING NEW RELATIONSHIPS

Paul writes, *"From now on...we regard no one from a [purely] human point of view..."*[22] In other words, we are to view new relationships through eyes of faith. Love is ever ready to believe the best,[23] so when we meet, I'm looking at what I *choose to believe* about you—your potential.

Now, believing and knowing are two different things. In the beginning, when I believe the best about you, I am completely open to you. I think that you're wonder-

---

22. 2 Corinthians 5:16, *AMP*
23. See 1 Corinthians 13:7, *AMP*

ful, and I'm one hundred percent committed to the relationship—until you begin to show me that you are not what you presented yourself to be. When that happens, I go from one hundred percent commitment to an eighty percent commitment. (As you can see, I am now beginning to have to protect myself, because our relationship is not manifesting what was originally understood between us.)

So, we have this relationship where I can be eighty percent invested, and everything is just fine, until a closer look at your life reveals more compromises; then we go from eighty to sixty—and then from sixty to forty, and so on.

> COMPROMISE IS REJECTED BY THOSE WHO CHOOSE TO LIVE IN EXCELLENCE — AND EXCELLENCE IS REJECTED BY THOSE WHO CHOOSE TO LIVE IN MEDIOCRITY.

What you believe about people is what causes you to come near to them, but the moment that you begin to take a look at them and discover that what you *believed* about them was incorrect, a repositioning must occur. Here is why: Excellence will refuse to compromise, and at the same time mediocrity will refuse to grow. *Compromise is rejected by those who choose to live in excellence—and excellence is rejected by those who choose to live in mediocrity.* So although you will experience the emotional pain of separation, it would not compare to the pain of knowing you had compromised your inner values.

The reason that a person *approaches* you is because of your advertisement; it's the fragrance and aroma that your life exudes. The reason that a person *stays* with you is the benefit that he gains from your relationship. He discovers, upon close examination, that you are genuinely found to be what you presented yourself to be.

James, the brother of Jesus, once said, *"Every good gift and every perfect gift is from above, and comes down from the Father of Lights, with whom is no variation or shadow of turning."*[24] The picture we get from this statement is that the closer we get to God, the better He looks. You can get close to Him, and He won't disappoint. You can get right up next to Him, crawl into His arms, and study the smallest little detail on His face. And the closer you get, the more wonderful will

---

24. James 1:17

> THE NECTAR
> OF A RELATIONSHIP
> WITH YOU MUST
> BE SWEETER THAN THE
> FRAGRANCE OF ITS
> ANNOUNCEMENT FROM YOU.

be the things you see—the sweeter He becomes.

The very same thing must be true about you—*the nectar of a relationship with you must be sweeter than the fragrance of its announcement from you.* As you present yourself to others in the best possible light, you try to show them that you are a particular kind of individual; the closer they get, the sweeter their experience with you must become.

THE GREENHOUSE PRINCIPLE

All relationships must be nurtured, but this is especially true of new relationships. When you decide that you want to pursue a relationship with a particular person whom you highly respect, you must be ready to invest substantial time, thought, and resources into your pursuit. Anything less than the conspicuous excellence of devoted attention and tireless servanthood, will delegate you to the throngs of other unnoticed people who would love to befriend such a person.

The way that a new relationship must be nurtured is very similar to the care and attention that a tiny, new plant must receive, in order to survive, and then thrive. It would be ridiculous to plant a fragile seedling out in the inclement weather among other established plants, and expect it to survive. A new seedling must be brought into the greenhouse and protected, until it is firmly rooted, and strong enough to withstand the storms that it will later need to endure.

New relationships need to be handled with the same devotion and attention. The foundation you build in the earliest stages of an association will establish the very nature and future of that relationship. The care and consideration given to an individual at the inception of the relationship will open the door to a strong, deeply rooted bond that will later be able to survive the assault of the most violent storms.

The quality of any relationship is completely dependent upon the level of pursuit that you can comfortably maintain. Many relationships seem to start out great in the beginning, only to fizzle out in the end. But once again I say, you must purpose to be *better* every time you are with someone. Most people 'put their best foot forward' at the beginning of a relationship, but then allow familiarity to sabotage their pursuit. You need to avoid that pitfall!

> THE QUALITY OF ANY RELATIONSHIP IS COMPLETELY DEPENDENT UPON THE LEVEL OF PURSUIT THAT YOU CAN COMFORTABLY MAINTAIN.

The passion of your pursuit must be noticeable. As you focus on adding value to this person's life, the mindfulness and attention that you give to each act of kindness communicates the *essence of exclusivity*; it reveals that this person is constantly in your thoughts, and you have done your homework to make a list of ways to please him. You are observant and vigilant, hearing what he says, but more importantly, *what he does not say*. You have studied the unique and specific contribution that you can make in this person's life. You have sown so much value into him that he is compelled to deepen his relationship with you. Your gift has now made room for you and brought you before great men.[25]

However, you must remember: though your gift *will make room for you*, your gift will not keep you there. You have to perform once you get there, doing what is required to *maintain* the relationship. Entering such an intense pursuit is not easy, and maintaining it even harder. Investing your life into another, to this degree, takes concentrated effort and hard work. But *nothing of any value comes easily.*

As you demonstrate your willingness to lay down your life to multiply greatness in the life of another, greatness will then begin to pursue you. Solomon confirmed this concept, when he said, *"Do you see a man who excels in his work? He will stand before kings; He will not stand before unknown men."*[26]

---

25. See Proverbs 18:16
26. Proverbs 22:29

EXCELLENT CHARACTER COMMANDS EXCLUSIVITY

Choosing a life of ease, comfort, compromise, or mediocrity does not develop the integrity and character needed to successfully pursue and attain the respect of great men. This kind of character is developed in the daily grind of *choosing* obedience instead of rebellion, discipline instead of self-indulgence, and service instead of being served. Excellent character is birthed out of the daily *choice* to do what is difficult but right, instead of what is easy but wrong. These choices include, most importantly, our relationships.

I don't know anyone in life *who wants* to associate themselves with people of questionable character. However, your primary focus must be the quality of *your character*. Once you have made your *own* character excellent, then you can require excellent character of others.

Many people who make good character a prerequisite for access into their lives (for example, friendship or marriage) would not even be able to pass their own character test! Solomon said that every man *proclaims* his own goodness, but a *truly faithful* man, is almost impossible to find.[27] He observed that it was easier for people to go with the flow, than to stand against the tide and to do what was right.

But then there are a few individuals that you hear about—the ones who stand out, because they are willing to stand against the crowd. They are the ones who are willing to put up with the pressure and rejection they get from others, because they are individuals of character.

The most important thing that you can ever do for yourself and for others is to be a person of unquestionable character. *God* is looking for a man or a woman of character. He's not looking for someone who wants to live in mediocrity or compromise.

There have been tremendously gifted men and women of God whose lives ended hideously, and we have discounted their greatness because of their "landing." Their ministries and, in some cases, even their lives ended *because of a lack of*

---

27. See Proverbs 20:6

character. Your excellent character will command respect; it cannot be ignored or denied. People will have to deal with it. You'll walk into a room and they'll think, "My God, this person, why do they irritate me so?"

It's your character. They are irritated not because you've done anything wrong, but because you've done *what is right,* and their own compromise begins to bother them. Your very presence says, "As long as I am here, we're going to do this the right way."

This is how your character will actually *cause* exclusivity to take place in your relationships. When you have developed your character to this degree and are not willing to forfeit your principles for anyone, others with excellent character will be drawn to you, and those who have chosen mediocrity will stay away. This will happen because *those who are comfortable in their compromise will never be comfortable in your excellence.*

It is at this point that exclusivity of relationship *chooses you,* for only those who are able to celebrate high standards and uncompromised principles will stick close to you.

You must remember, *there is safety in selectivity.* In relationship, you must embrace what is wise, reject what is foolish, and contribute what is uniquely and specifically your own. You must protect the circle of Godly associations in your life by valuing integrity and principle above *any*

> THOSE WHO
> ARE COMFORTABLE
> IN THEIR COMPROMISE WILL
> NEVER BE COMFORTABLE
> IN YOUR EXCELLENCE.

relationship. Finally, you must value yourself enough to qualify your friendships. By applying the Law of Exclusivity in your life, you will be preserved, protected, and kept free from entanglements that have been assigned to destroy you and your assignment.

THE LAW OF EXCLUSIVITY

Authentic commitment
demands selectivity, not inclusivity.

+ Inspiration is the discovery of options, while focus is the elimination of them.
+ A double standard is only acceptable to a hypocrite.
+ At any given moment, every relationship is either taking you closer to or further from God.
+ If you desire to be great, you must qualify for access to the great.
+ It is impossible for my gift to change the quality of another man's heart.
+ Compromise is the willingness to accept what you don't believe, because you are unwilling to stand for what you do.
+ Giants left undefeated will ultimately end in your demise.
+ Whatever you compromise to keep, you will eventually lose.
+ You cannot experience freedom without gratitude.
+ If I am a true friend, I must never fear others more than I love you.
+ Neutrality is the surrender of responsibility.
+ What you believe about a person causes you to come to them, but what you know about a person causes you to stay with them.
+ Compromise is rejected by those who choose to live in excellence–and excellence is rejected by those who choose to live in mediocrity.
+ The nectar of a relationship with you must be sweeter than the fragrance of its announcement from you.
+ The quality of any relationship is completely dependent upon the level of pursuit that you can comfortably maintain.
+ Those who are comfortable in their compromise will never be comfortable in your excellence.

MY QUALIFICATIONS FOR FRIENDSHIP

Number 1: My friends must be committed to long-lasting relationships.

Number 2: My friends must have empires within them.

Number 3: My friends must be sowers.

Number 4: My friends must qualify to receive my seed.

Number 5: My friends must prize integrity above relationship.

Number 6: My friends must be willing to confront my enemies.

THE LAW OF
TRANSPARENCY

COMPLETE DISCLOSURE
IS AN INDISPENSABLE CHARACTERISTIC
OF ALL MEANINGFUL RELATIONSHIPS.

6

COMPLETE DISCLOSURE IS AN INDISPENSABLE CHARACTERISTIC OF ALL MEANINGFUL RELATIONSHIPS.

Transparency is somewhat of a buzzword these days. In fact, it even made 'word of the year' recently. The Encarta World English Dictionary has two applicable meanings: *to be clearly recognizable for what it, he, or she really is,* and *to be completely open and frank about things.* A contemporary meaning for the word is simply, "Full disclosure!"

Healthy relationships are transparent relationships. In other words, full disclosure is expected in meaningful relationships, and the delectable reward of full disclosure is intimacy.

GETTING HONEST WITH YOURSELF

Transparency begins by being honest with one's self. The person in your life who is most susceptible to deception is *you.* Often, everyone else will get more truth from you than you are willing to give yourself. Even when deception is exposed, it is common to respond with, "Well, God knows my heart."

Yes, God knows your heart. But let's read what He said about it, through the prophet Jeremiah, *"The heart is deceitful above all things and desperately wicked. Who can know it?"*[1]

> NO ACCOMPLISHMENT
> IS EVER REWARDED
> AS A RESULT OF
> GOOD INTENTIONS.

If you *really* want to know what's inside your heart, listen to your mouth and watch what you do. Don't try to subjectively evaluate what is in your heart. It's too easy to give yourself extra credit for your *intentions.*

Remember: *No accomplishment is ever rewarded as a result of good intentions.*

Until your life is tried and tested, you'll never know who you are. That's the reason that you need to look into your life and see what you've *done,* not what you *think* you've done. Most people *think* that they are more truthful, more loyal, more committed, and more transparent than they really are. In fact, you're really *not* who you feel that you are. Surprised? Well, stay with me as I explain further.

"Well, I'm a man of integrity," you might protest.

Why is it, then, that there are times when folks get into business with you, and complain about your business ethics?

"Well, I'm a person of great dignity," you might say.

Then, have you paid back, *on time,* the money that you have owed to everyone? Does failure to keep your word sound like dignity?

Friend, you are not a person of integrity because **you** say that you are; you are a person of integrity because **someone else** says that you are. You are not a person who is fair because you say it; rather, you are a person who is fair because *others* say that you are. *"Don't praise yourself; let others do it!"*[2] They are much more able to give an accurate assessment of who you really are.

Beware of the common trap of self-deception. Let me give you three reasons for self-deception:

1. Jeremiah 17:9
2. Proverbs 27:2, *NLT*

1. An *over*-inflated opinion about oneself

2. An *under*-inflated opinion about oneself, or more commonly known as low self-esteem.

Interestingly, both of these first conditions stem from pride, because they are birthed from a *selfish focus*. A selfish focus cannot foster truth within you, because *you are not the source of truth*. When you enter the realm of selfishness, you automatically open the door to all kinds of self-deception.

The third reason for self-deception is:

3. Ignorance: Through the prophet Hosea, God said, *"My people are destroyed for a lack of knowledge..."*[3]

Ignorance actually has two sides:

a. Ignorance from a lack of awareness—This is the individual who just *does not know*. To be ignorant basically means that one is not aware of something. I used to believe that this was the case for most people. But, more and more every day, I do not believe that people are as unknowing as they pretend to be. The great majority fit into the next category.

b. Ignorance from a deliberate disdain for truth—This individual *chooses to ignore* the truth. He *ignores* what he already knows.

Honesty is demanded of you, if you are ever going to fulfill your purpose and vision in life. How are you ever going to get anywhere if you are not willing to face off with yourself? You must tell *yourself* the truth first.

One of the greatest days of my life was the day that I got honest with myself, and came face to face with my own self-deception. I was finally willing to take a truthful look at myself and say, "This stuff needs to change." I came to the realization that *I can never change what I am unwilling to face.*

That's why I live my life in front of people. I'm not hiding anything. I am willing to be transparent, and when necessary, I will tell on myself. Every once in a while, I look at myself in the mirror, point my finger at me, and say, "I'm tellin' on you, you're bad!" Now, other people wouldn't think what I did was bad, but I do, because I know best when I have compromised. I choose to live far inside the

---

3. Hosea 4:6

> **I CAN NEVER CHANGE WHAT I AM UNWILLING TO FACE.**

boundaries of truth and virtue. We must continually pursue truth and transparency. How does someone pursue truth? By filling his soul with truth. Any good that happens in your life, at all, happens by inner prosperity. When your soul is prospering in an area, that prosperity will permeate from the inside out. You'll push whatever is on the inside of you to the outside of your life. What's inside of you *will* manifest. So, if you want to change what you see on the outside, don't attempt to do it with an outside "fix"; *continually look within,* and become honest and transparent with yourself.

So, you can see that change is a two-step process:

1. To accurately **assess** what is presently inside our hearts, we must examine the *outside* of our lives, *observing what we say and do.*

2. To **change** traits that we don't like, we must examine the *inside* of our lives and *displace the lies with the truth.*

When integrity and truth become the abundance of your heart, and your mouth begins to speak from that abundance, then integrity and truth will be the earmarks of every situation you touch.

GETTING HONEST WITH OTHERS

Don't be misled into thinking that dishonesty is just a private issue between you and God. The Apostle Paul clearly said, *"We must provide that which is honest not only in the sight of God, but also in the sight of men."*[4] We have to be honest, truthful, and transparent in the sight of people, not just in the sight of God.

Have you ever encountered an individual who changed his opinions or viewpoints, based upon whomever he happened to be with at any particular instant? Like a chameleon changing color to match its environment, this type of person

---

4. Romans 12:17 *KJV,* author's paraphrase

believes that by agreeing with *every* person he talks to, he will be accepted by all and confronted by none.

It is almost impossible to form any kind of trusting relationship with such a volatile person, for you are constantly wondering if he is undermining you behind your back today, for something that he heartily agreed with you about yesterday![5] The Apostle Paul called this type of person "double-tongued".[6]

The Greek word for "double-tongued" is the compound word *dilogos*, which can be translated *two-worded*. It is the picture of *a man or woman who says one thing to one person but a different thing to the next.*[7] This is usually indicative of an extremely insecure person who is driven by the need to please everyone. The problem is he ends up irritating and alienating everyone, because he has absolutely no integrity and cannot be trusted.

FIVE CANONS OF TRANSPARENCY

Let's look at five canons of transparency:

1. Straight-forwardness

James, the brother of Jesus, once stated that the wisdom that comes from heaven is "...*without partiality and without hypocrisy.*"[8] We often speak of someone who is hypocritical as being "two-faced;" however the Greek word for hypocrisy has a very interesting and descriptive meaning. It gives us the picture of *someone who speaks from behind a mask.*

I'm fairly certain that each one of us has, at one point in our lives, been on one side of that mask or the other. Have you ever presented yourself to be one thing on the outside, knowing deep in your heart that you were something else entirely? Have you ever plastered a smile on your face and forced yourself to be civil to someone, when inside you were seething over how unjustly they had treated you?

Maybe you've had someone treat you like his very best friend one day, only to

5. Rick Renner, *Sparkling Gems from the Greek* (Tulsa, OK: Teach All Nations, 2003), p. 693.
6. See 1 Timothy 3:8
7. Ibid, Renner.
8. James 3:17

have that same person stab you in the back and spread vicious rumors about you the next? Or are you a business owner who, in good faith, hired an employee based upon his credentials, only to discover that this person misrepresented himself and has been embezzling funds from your company? People such as this have made duplicity and hypocrisy a lifestyle; these individuals are filled with treachery and *guile*.

Jesus called Andrew, "...*an Israelite...in whom [there] is no guile.*"[9] Guile is an interesting term. It goes much deeper than telling a lie. You can actually lie and not really be a person of guile. Guile is a whole character package of deceit. Guile gives us the picture that the internal seat and governor of a person's life *has become crooked*. Andrew, however, was *straight forward*, honest, open, and transparent.

A person of guile is one who has systematically become both the deceived and the deceiver. He has created a framework of lies that he has told himself so repeatedly, that he believes these lies to be the truth. This framework of lies is *his truth*, and he is convinced that his viewpoint is how things really are.

An individual with a character of guile is a fraudulent person, a double-talker. He actually speaks well of you when in front of you, but behind your back, he leaves little hints of doubt and uncertainty about you. He may not even *say* anything to specifically undermine you, but he manages to plant seeds of distrust about you in the minds of others.

Hypocrisy and deception encompass and define everything about a person of guile—his whole genre, his mannerisms, his life style. He "believes his own press releases," as the cliché goes. He is skeptical and suspicious of everyone but himself, and judges every matter from his perspective alone.

Dealing with someone who "speaks from behind a mask" can be disappointing and hurtful, even in casual associations; but it is especially devastating when you have already deeply invested into the relationship. There are not many things on earth that are more painful than having to endure the agony of betrayed intimacy.

This is why the laws of relationship discussed in this book are so important. These laws are put in place to *filter and qualify* every relationship, and hopefully to expose and disqualify those who are "speaking from behind a mask," before too

9. John 1:47, *KJV*

much damage is done. You must pass every relationship through this filtering process, because it is crucial that, at some point, you develop the kind of intimate relationships where you can be absolutely transparent, honest, and vulnerable, without the slightest hesitation or twinge of fear.

2. Intimacy

Why is the quest for intimacy so crucial? Why is it so important that we have at least a few relationships that are profoundly intimate? Because, man was made for intimacy. Intimacy was on the Father's mind when He created mankind. The call of intimacy is what moved Him, throughout generations of wickedness, to extend mercy to any who were sincerely penitent. And it was His burning desire for intimacy with mankind that inspired His marvelous plan of salvation.

This is why I believe that the sweetest and most aromatic nectar will be drawn only from a truly intimate relationship with those who are already deeply intimate with the Heavenly Father. This kind of private tenderness and secret warmth of devotion toward God, *through a human relationship*, is the closest thing to heaven on earth that any individual will ever experience.

This depth of transparency is precious and uncommon in today's dysfunctional society, but it is precisely this kind of fellowship for which we were designed. We must pursue it and search for it as for a rare treasure, and when found, protect it as we would protect life itself.

3. Vulnerability

There are many who will argue that seeking deep transparency and intimacy is ill advised at best and dangerous at worst. Vulnerability is seen as a weakness, exposing one to needless pain and heartache. Innocence is believed to be a detriment, making one susceptible to attack and trespass.

But, unless we become vulnerable, we will essentially cease to live. Unless we celebrate and preserve innocence in our hearts and souls, we will develop stony hearts of cynicism and be suspicious of every kindness. *Unless we tear down the walls of self-protection, we will never experience the sublime joy of being protected.*

Building a fortress around your heart *will*, indeed, prevent you from ever being hurt again; but it will also prevent you from ever giving or receiving love again. Without love, the human heart shrivels up and dies, for it was *for love* that the human heart was created. Yes, it takes great courage to choose, one more time, to become open and transparent—especially if your heart was trampled the last time you made that choice. But if you want to *live*, rather than merely *exist*, is there really any other choice?

> UNLESS WE TEAR DOWN
> THE WALLS OF
> SELF-PROTECTION,
> WE WILL NEVER
> EXPERIENCE
> THE SUBLIME JOY
> OF BEING PROTECTED.

Vulnerability is a position of strength, not of weakness. It is a weak, fearful person who will shrink away from intimacy and commitment. He will say, in the words of an old song, "I am a rock—I am an island...A rock feels no pain—And an island never cries..."[10] But it is a strong, faith-filled person who will choose transparency, vulnerability, and commitment, knowing that the bliss of intimacy and love is worth the risk of pain and tears. For this love between us is God's desire. It is from this position of strength that life-long dreams are realized and God-given visions are manifested.

4. Truth and Honesty

The word "truth" comes from the Hebrew word *"emeth"*, which means *stable, certain, right, and sure.* Another form of the word is derived from the Hebrew *"aman"*, which means *to build up, to support, or to foster.* Interestingly, the word truth means *to foster as a parent or to foster as a nurse.* It means *to be firm and faithful, permanent and steadfast, established and verifiable.*[11] Truthfulness is to come into agreement with an indisputable standard.

Truth infers loyalty and trustworthiness. It implies sincerity and genuineness. Rare it is to find a person with a warmth and genuineness about them, someone who is truly interested in others and expresses that involvement with their words.

A very simple definition of honesty is *behavior in action and words that aims to convey the truth.* It is a quality that is essential if one is going to live a happy and

10. Simon and Garfunkel, *Sounds of Silence*, "I Am A Rock", (New York, NY: Columbia Records, CBS, Inc., 1966).
11. James Strong, *The New Strong's Exhaustive Concordance of the Bible/Dictionary of the Hebrew Bible* (Nashville, TN: Thomas Nelson Publishers, 1990) p. 1122/14.

healthy life, and it is *required* of those whom God calls His people.

Conversely, dishonesty is *a way of speaking or acting that leads people to the place of being misled.* It lures them to the place of being deceived or deluded to the point where they are being cheated out of something that belongs to them in the relationship.

> NEVER PRESENT YOURSELF, *EXTERNALLY,* WHAT YOU ARE NOT, *INTERNALLY.*

Never present yourself, *externally,* what you are not, *internally.* Intimacy in relationship is impossible without honesty and truthfulness. In a transparent relationship, honesty and truth are celebrated, nurtured, and protected. The "inside information" that comes from full disclosure is **never**—let me repeat—**never** revealed to others or used as a weapon against the one who exposed his vulnerability to you. Those moments of pure trust and spiritual/emotional nakedness are the precious building materials of a cherished relationship.

The ancient Israelite King David, after becoming vulnerable and transparent with the man of God and realizing his sin, implored God for pardon and cleansing:

> Behold, you desire truth in the inward parts, and in the hidden part You will make me to know wisdom. Purge me with hyssop, and I shall be clean. Wash me, and I shall be whiter than snow. Make me hear joy and gladness, that the bones You have broken may rejoice. Hide your face from my sins, and blot out all my iniquities. Create in me a clean heart, O God, and renew a steadfast spirit within me. Do not cast me away from Your presence, and do not take Your Holy Spirit from me. Restore to me the joy of Your salvation, and uphold me by Your generous Spirit.[12]

> He said, "Against you and you only have I sinned and done this evil in your sight."[13]

David came to the full-blown realization that, *"Surely you desire truth in the inward parts."*

Friend, you have to understand that in our society, where we are bombarded with ethical relativism and situational ethics, the foundational pillars of truth and

12. Psalm 51:6-12
13. Psalm 51:4

honesty are severely threatened. If these foundational pillars are removed, the very structure of our civilization will collapse in a heap of ruins.

Many people have become masters at avoiding or distorting the truth, because they refuse to acknowledge God. Their attitudes are like that of Pilot, who mocked Jesus when he said, "...*What is truth?...*"[14] He sneeringly insinuated, "Go ahead and tell me what the truth is; because in this situation, *I'm* the truth."

Jesus said, "You would have no power at all, if it wasn't given to you from above!" Basically, "Hey Pilot, if I wanted to play a power game with you, this would be over right now."

You see, even in Christendom, friend, we play the game. We've all heard the phrase "there is 'honor' among thieves." Well, there's that "false honor" among Christians, as well. It's an unspoken understanding that says, "We're not going to discuss the real issues. And as long as all of us do not discuss the real issues, the real issues do not exist." **But that's not true.** Those issues *do* exist. Many times we fool ourselves and *call it walking in love,* not realizing that *we are consenting to another's death.*

> WE FOOL OURSELVES AND CALL IT WALKING IN LOVE, NOT REALIZING THAT WE ARE CONSENTING TO ANOTHER'S DEATH.

We all have weaknesses and flaws—even if we want to avoid them, discount them, or pretend they do not exist. It doesn't matter what we do, because the truth is a constant, unchanging standard that continues throughout time. Divine principles don't slide up and down a scale, like the ever-changing scale of man's viewpoints and opinions. *You must guard integrity with your life, for it is better to die defending the truth than to live in the bondage of deceit.*

Solomon, the wisest man in ancient Israel, implored, "*Buy the truth, and do not sell it...*"[15] Truth is such an invaluable commodity that wise people will pay whatever it costs to attain it. No expense is too high, no sacrifice too dear. You must gladly buy the whole field, in order to get the pearl of truth. And once the purity of truth has been tasted, it must not be sold or relinquished for any price.

14. John 18:38
15. Proverbs 23:23

5. Absolute Integrity

If any kind of meaningful, long-term relationship is to be built with someone, it will take integrity—not simply as a *preference*, but as a *requirement*. If you can't be trusted with the small things, *you can't be trusted at all.*

> GUARD INTEGRITY
> WITH YOUR LIFE,
> FOR IT IS BETTER TO DIE
> DEFENDING THE TRUTH
> THAN TO LIVE IN
> THE BONDAGE OF DECEIT.

Integrity is displayed when what you say and what you do are the same. This is the simplest definition of integrity. Integrity will protect you and firmly establish confidence in your reliability.

Integrity and reliability are vital for *both* personal and business success. The UCLA Graduate School of Management and Korn/Ferry International of New York City conducted a joint study of 1,300 senior executives, asking them to identify the trait most needed to prosper and succeed in business. Seventy-one percent of them felt that *integrity* was that essential trait. And a study by the Center for Creative Research found that in spite of the numerous obstacles and mistakes that were successfully overcome by ambitious, corporate-climbing executives, anyone who compromised principle and integrity, by betraying a trust, had no further

> IF YOU CAN'T
> BE TRUSTED WITH
> THE SMALL THINGS, YOU
> CAN'T BE TRUSTED AT ALL.

advancements in his career with the organization.[16]

When guiding and supervising people, it didn't matter how effective the people management skills were, if they were used without integrity, sincerity, or an altruistic motive, one was seen as manipulative, and rightly so.

You need to be an individual whose viewpoints, management skills, and personal ethics are based upon the firm and unchanging foundation of Divine precepts, not the ever-fluctuating opinions of men. Your decision to live by principle MUST be made *before* the temptations ever arise to break that principle. And it is this type of principled person that you should pursue in your relationships,

---

16. John C. Maxwell, *Relationships 101-What Every Leader Needs To Know* (Nashville. TN: Thomas Nelson Publishers, 2003), p. 56.

> **YOUR INTEGRITY WILL PRESERVE YOU; BUT IT WILL ALSO PRESERVE OTHERS.**

because then there will be no guesswork in discerning motives, and no tip-toeing around forbidden or off-limit issues.

Your integrity will preserve *you*; but it will also preserve *others*. When you walk in integrity, others can trust your intentions and motives, and open themselves up to the benefits of a transparent relationship with you. They know you'll not harm them, because they have observed that whether you are with them or apart from them, you will consistently live by principle.

THE POWER OF TRUTH

There is great power in truth. Truth has the power to do the following things in our lives:

* **Truth brings us into our relationship with God.**[17] — Only by truth can we know God, for God *is* truth, in His very essence.

* **Truth brings us into the light.**[18] — If you are beginning to get frustrated about seeing honest people denigrated, and deceitful people getting away with so much, just remember the day is coming when *every* man's actions and motives will be brought out into the light. *He that does the truth, it will come to the light.*

* **Truth purifies our soul.**[19] — The cleansing ability of truth is enormous. Truth has the power to separate us from anything that would degrade or shame us. When a person embraces integrity, he begins to walk in dignity, security, and confidence.

* **Truth makes us free.**[20] — You can almost visibly see if a person is walking in truth or not. When someone is bound up and inhibited, or has a poor attitude, it's a good indication of a lack of truth in his life.

---

17. See James 1:18
18. See John 3:21
19. See 1 Peter 1:22
20. See John 8:32

THE LAW OF TRANSPARENCY | 149

* **Truth leads us in the right way.**[21] — It is a lamp to our feet and a light to our path.[22]

* **Truth preserves leaders.**[23] — If you are a leader, you are a target. There are many forces that want to take you out. Nothing matches the protective power of truth. When the accusations are flying, and the spotlight of incrimination is turned upon you, there is nothing as assuring and secure as being on the side of truth.

BENEFITS OF TRANSPARENCY

Relationships are progressive in all aspects. As commitment increases, responsibilities increase—but so also do the benefits. Transparency will bring special benefits that will propel a relationship to a whole new level of intimacy and value. Let's examine the benefits of living transparently in relationship.

1. Purity of Motive

Suspicions of ulterior motives are sacrificed on the altar of transparency. Transparency means *nothing is hidden*; therefore, there are no hidden agendas. If I have pursued a relationship with you, my reasons for doing so are laid bare before you, open to your scrutiny and examination.

Those who cannot be transparent and straightforward will find it difficult to cultivate meaningful relationships. An unwillingness to be forthright implies dishonesty, and no benefits can be gained through dishonesty. Without openness and integrity, everything that's given to you will fall through the crack of *insincere or false motive.*

People sometimes tell me, "I really believed that individual was a good person —but I was so wrong."

My response is, "You just didn't give it enough time."

In time, whatever is hidden in there comes out. John wrote, *"But those who do what is right come to the light gladly, so everyone can see that they are doing what*

---

21. See Psalm 43:3; John 16:13
22. See Psalm 119:105
23. See Proverbs 20:28

God wants."[24] If an individual is doing what is right, transparency and openness are his friends, not his enemies. He is eager for full disclosure, for it confirms his pure motive.

Always learn how to wait until the smoke clears. You will be able to clearly see the individual who is spreading seeds of doubt and discord. You will also be able to clearly see the one who is eager to live candidly and openly before all men—the one with nothing to hide.

2. Restored Innocence

There is no clearer picture of purity and innocence than that of the first man and woman in the Garden of Eden. Nothing dark or evil had yet invaded their guileless, childlike hearts. But then, the Liar slithered in to sow his poison.

"God is not being open and transparent with you," he said. "He is hiding good things from you...He is withholding wisdom from you...You can be as gods if you'll just listen to me."[25]

After the man and the woman disobeyed God in the garden, they realized that they were naked. When they heard the voice of God coming in the cool of the day, they made aprons from fig leaves, covered up their loins, and ran and hid. Why did they hide? Because *disobedience causes an immediate withdrawal from intimacy.*

> DISOBEDIENCE CAUSES AN IMMEDIATE WITHDRAWAL FROM INTIMACY.

When you talk about intimacy, some people immediately think of it as a sexual issue. Intimacy, however, is an honesty issue. Adam and Eve attempted to hide from God because *they did not want to be transparent with Him.* This is the very same test that you and I face every day. Are we going to be transparent, or are we going to try to "sew up some fig leaves" and hide, to avoid intimacy?

One of the greatest people that you can ever meet inside of your life is a person that you can be truly open with. It is a rare thing to actually find someone who continues to love, respect, and celebrate you when you are completely transparent with him. When you discover someone like this, you don't have to

24. John 3:21, *NLT*
25. See Genesis 3:4-5

continually rebuild the relationship every time that you get together, because you've already established certain criteria for the relationship. You've established trust and confidence, and you don't have to spar any more. You've passed the test of whether or not you want to be together, and you can now build your relationship on the strength of openness, vulnerability, and restored innocence.

Those who live their lives in complete honesty are *joyful, childlike people.*[26] Their hearts are pure and clean, not burdened down with the baggage of duplicity. They do not put up appearances or deceptive fronts. They are not concerned or fearful that someone may catch them in a lie.

Transparency creates child-like innocence. You become unencumbered by the fear of rejection and uninhibited in demonstrations of affection. And as with a child, others respond to your purity and innocence with genuine tenderness and favor.

3. Unfeigned Love

Peter, one of Jesus' disciples, exhorted, *"Seeing ye have purified your souls in obeying the truth through the Spirit unto **unfeigned love** of the brethren, see that ye love one another with a pure heart fervently."*[27] Love that is "unfeigned" is love that is pure, sincere, and without hypocrisy. This is the type of love that a transparent relationship yields.

Actually, love that is tentative and vacillating is not love at all. It is manipulation; it promises fulfillment and acceptance, but never truly delivers. Real love is not disingenuous and two-faced, withholding itself when annoyed or provoked. Instead:

Love endures long and is patient and kind; love never is envious nor boils over with jealousy, is not boastful or vainglorious, does not display itself haughtily.

It is not conceited (arrogant and inflated with pride); it is not rude (unmannerly) and does not act unbecomingly. Love (God's love in us) does not insist on its own rights or its own way, for it is not self-seeking; it is not touchy or fretful or resentful; it takes no account of the evil done to it [it pays no attention to a suffered wrong].

It does not rejoice at injustice and unrighteousness, but rejoices when right and truth prevail.

26. See Psalm 32:1-2, *NLT*
27. 1 Peter 1:22, *KJV*

Love bears up under anything and everything that comes, is ever ready to believe the best of every person, its hopes are fadeless under all circumstances, and it endures everything [without weakening].

Love never fails [never fades out or becomes obsolete or comes to an end].[28]

Unfeigned love is full of compassion. True love and compassion are not merely superficial sympathy. Compassion means that you treat the situation as if *you* were the one going through it. You are willing to share in the heartache and pain of another. This kind of empathy and tenderness is the product of relational transparency.

Compassion is a rare find. There are a lot of people who can muster up sympathy for others, but very few people know what true compassion really is. Having a bleeding heart for a lost cause is not genuine compassion. Compassion says, "I want to feel what you feel. I want to deal with what you deal with. How can I relieve your pain? How can I bring restoration and erase the shame? Please let me lift your weight and share the crushing burden. Don't endure this alone."

As you pursue genuine love and transparency in your relationships, you will begin to take on the responsibility of becoming a shock absorber in the life of your friend, even when you don't feel like it or your friend doesn't receive it. You will find yourself striving to answer questions that others are not even willing to ask or acknowledge. You will yearn to silence the roar of years of disappointment in their life, and help remove the obstacles, so they can be repositioned to win.

4. Unquestioned Trust

No man or woman on earth was designed to survive or succeed alone. Rich and prosperous is the person who has nurtured such intimacy in his relationships that he can relish the benefits of placing unquestioned trust in them.

One of the greatest problems that you face in your life is that *you trust yourself too much.* What's the main difference between a person who fails and a person who succeeds? One is willing to face his shortcomings. The successful individual thinks, "You know, I'm going to get some help with this situation, because I don't trust '*me*.'"

How transparent are you willing to be with someone whom you say that you

---

28. 1 Corinthians 13:4-8, *AMP*

trust? Are you making yourself vulnerable to correction and change, or are you fearfully cloaking areas of your life in self-protection? You need to recognize that *fear is the proof of a lack of trust.*

Inside your life, you've got to come to the place where you have someone that you trust implicitly. If that person ever told you that you did, in fact, blunder, your

> **FEAR IS THE PROOF OF A LACK OF TRUST.**

response would be, "OK, I believe that I did it, *because you said that I did*; I trust you, because I know you wouldn't lie to me. You wouldn't hurt me."

Who is that person in your life? In most cases, *you* are the only one that you trust to that degree, even though you are the one who lies to yourself more than anyone else in the world.

In evaluating my own heart, in the arena of trust, I developed a personal checklist that I would like to share with you. Look into a mirror and pose these questions to yourself:

* ***Do I ask others to point out my blind spots?***

   By blind spots, I refer to those things that you do, that you don't know that you do. There are things that have happened inside of your life, and you have no idea the extent to which they are affecting you. That is why they are called blind spots! Think about it. A blind spot is only blind to the one who has it. You have to be willing to trust someone enough that if they point out a weakness or a flaw to you, you will step up and take responsibility for it, just because *you trust.*

* ***Am I willing to confront these blind spots?***

   You have to determine to be courageous enough to not only acknowledge the blind spots, but to face them head-on and deal with them. Face your past and deal with the weakness in your life. This will likely be a daily discipline. Be willing to look your weaknesses square in the eyes, and declare, "You will *not* control me. You will *not* have me at the end of the day. You will *not* win these hours from me." Every day, that is your choice.

* ***Do I deceive myself into believing that I'm more than what I really am?***

   Do you think of yourself more highly than you should? Knowing who you are is only half of it; you must also know who you are not. A lot of individuals get real cocky when they discover who they are. They get into pride and arrogance over who they are, never even considering that they need to embrace vulnerability and trust in others because of who they're *not*.

* ### *Do I exaggerate my own abilities?*

Bragging and exaggeration are classic symptoms of low self-esteem and puny productivity. Often, we exaggerate our abilities, because we are embarrassed about our lack of the same. Allow a trusted friend or mentor to shine the light of truth upon this flaw. He will love you enough to not only speak the truth, but to do so in love. Then, he will love you enough to hold you accountable for your deliverance from this problem.

* ### *Do I tell half-truths?*

We do this to escape consequences or for self-protection, not knowing that we are actually lying with our mouths closed! If you withhold pertinent information in order to tilt a situation in your favor, you have just committed a *lie of omission*. These half-truths can be even more damaging than out-right lies, especially to your own conscience. Why? Because you can rationally convince yourself that you told the truth, when your heart knows it was *tainted truth*. Nothing hardens a heart or sears a conscience quicker that *tainted truth*. Transparency in relationship will protect you from this surreptitious form of dishonesty.

* ### *Do I flatter people to gain their approval?*

Let me first ask this—Do you realize that if you do not forcibly solve problems, make people feel good about their day, keep yourself from misunderstandings, and so on, that you have become a problem?

You're either a problem solver or you are a problem. You will only be remembered for the problems you create or the problems you solve.[29] So, you need to do all that you can to be pleasing to your superiors. Become the "teacher's pet!" However, you must not *flatter*, in order to gain approval.

The difference between flattery and a compliment is so slight, you will never hear it; you will only see it. An individual who flatters someone else to get somewhere is *defrauding*—he is taking something from that person. An individual who compliments a person is not taking something from a person, but instead, giving something to a person. The two can *sound*

29. Mike Murdock, *Seeds of Wisdom on Your Assignment* (Denton, TX: The Wisdom Center, 2001), p. 2.

exactly the same, in words, but their *motives are different.* Again, strive for transparency, because transparency exposes motives.

* **Do I give damaging reports of others in order to make myself look good?**
If the only way you are able to look good in the eyes of others is to make someone else look bad, you have much work to do in discovering the unique and special person that God created you to be. In assassinating the character of someone else, you are exposing the lack of character in yourself.

> YOU WILL
> ONLY BE REMEMBERED
> FOR THE PROBLEMS
> YOU CREATE OR THE
> PROBLEMS YOU SOLVE.

Do the hard work of being brutally honest with yourself and others. Choose, *on purpose,* to expose your insecurities to a trusted mentor or friend. Remember this: You will never grow until you choose to become vulnerable and receptive to change. Truthfulness will thrust you to freedom.

Unless you are willing to trust someone enough to allow them to tell you the truth, you will not overcome the developmental impasse you face today. Trust is an indispensable part of any meaningful relationship.

5. Unwavering Confidence

The intimacy level of every relationship will be tested, in large part, by the level of transparency that each party is willing to walk in. *Transparency fear-proofs a relationship.* If someone has been absolutely transparent with me, fear will find no place to insert its ugly fangs. And when fear is shut out-of-doors, confidence and faith reign supreme.

Confidence or <u>confide</u>-ence is gained when the secret intimacies of the heart are mutually disclosed and protected. We have each shared with one whom we trust will never harm nor betray. Because of the tested and proven integrity of the relationship, confidence is sure, true, and unwavering, giving rise to further transparency and deeper intimacy.

> TRANSPARENCY
> FEAR-PROOFS
> A RELATIONSHIP.

Full disclosure demonstrates your utter trust in another's ability to love and protect. Indeed, relational transparency cultivates intimacy and favor. This gift of intimacy is the highest form of confidence and respect that one can show another. It is a holy gift, and blessed is the person to whom it is entrusted.

THE LAW OF TRANSPARENCY

Complete disclosure is an indispensable characteristic
of all meaningful relationships.

→ No accomplishment is ever rewarded as a result of good intentions.

→ I can never change what I am unwilling to face.

→ Unless we tear down the walls of self-protection, we will never experience the sublime joy of being protected.

→ Never present yourself, *externally*, what you are not, *internally*.

→ We fool ourselves and call it walking in love, not realizing that we are consenting to another's death.

→ Guard integrity with your life, for it is better to die defending the truth than to live in the bondage of deceit.

→ If you can't be trusted with the small things, you can't be trusted at all.

→ Your integrity will preserve *you*, but it will also preserve *others*.

→ Disobedience causes an immediate withdrawal from intimacy.

→ Fear is the proof of a lack of trust.

→ You will only be remembered for the problems you create or the problems you solve.

→ Transparency fear-proofs a relationship.

THE LAW OF
MUTUAL
BENEFIT

THE QUALITY OF ANY RELATIONSHIP
IS COMPLETELY DEPENDENT UPON THE
WILLINGNESS OF MUTUAL PURSUIT.

7

THE QUALITY OF ANY RELATIONSHIP

IS COMPLETELY DEPENDENT UPON

THE WILLINGNESS OF MUTUAL PURSUIT.

Meaningful relationship is only possible when respect, honor, and value are mutually shared. One-sided relationships do not last. If one person is always the pursuer/giver, and the other is always the receiver of that pursuit, the relationship will eventually crumble. For any relationship to endure and improve, there must be give-and-take, so that the benefits of the relationship are available to all.

The very word 'relationship' *implies* involvement by *both* parties. A one-sided pursuit does not even qualify as a *relationship*. A true relationship is the state of being *mutually connected*. The lines of connection run both ways, with both parties participating in both giving and receiving.

Mutual benefit is the result of mutual obligation. When *both* individuals enter the relationship with only the thought of *giving*, they will both end up being receivers. What I, personally, plan on bringing to any relationship is *give/give*, not give/take. When the other person enters the relationship feeling the same duty and responsibility to *give/give*, the benefits for both of us will be abundant, and there will be no lack.

This reciprocity, this interdependence and complementary exchange, becomes *impossible* if you have entered relationship with a *professional taker*. Regretfully, our society today is replete with depraved individuals who make it their sole aim to merely *use* their relationships to feed their own greed and perverted lusts.

This is why it is so critical that you form the right relationships early in life. Your future will be built or destroyed by the relationships that you nurture. Your life's purpose rests on whether you cultivate relationships with givers or with takers.

WHY PEOPLE SEEK RELATIONSHIPS

The aura of excellence and success is tremendously magnetic. People are drawn to the virtue that lives on the inside of individuals who live excellently. Others want what they have, and will therefore begin to follow them. But overall, I have observed two main reasons why people follow someone:

1. People will follow you because they want want *to learn* what you've mastered.

2. People will follow you because they want *to take* what you've got.

The people that are magnetically drawn to your excellence fall into one of two categories—the *takers* or the *givers*.

You will have to discern the motives of the people who are coming toward you, by asking this question: Why do they want to be around me? Find out *why* someone is pursuing you and why he wants to be your friend. Remember, every person that's around you will actually *add* to your life, or *subtract from* it.

Let's say that you talk to several people today. Each one of them has a purpose in speaking with you; but when your conversation is over, you will either be better or worse for having spoken with them. In every encounter you have, you'll either get a load added to your life "backpack" or have weights removed from it.

You have to be able to determine what each individual is doing, and conduct that relationship accordingly.

When the right people are in your life, you will be able to grow and focus on your assignment. When the wrong people are in your life, they will cause you to focus on them and their problems. The result is that neither of you will grow.

GIVERS AND TAKERS

Let's now examine the motives, attitudes, and actions of givers and takers. In doing this comparative study, it is my hope that you will search your own heart, give yourself an honest appraisal, and assess in which category you fall. Remember, relationships will eventually disintegrate if one or both parties are takers. If you seem to have consistent problems within your relationships, you need to evaluate whether you have been contributing to them or leeching from them.

I would also encourage you to scrutinize each of your associations to determine if you are in relationship with a giver or with a taker. If you find that you are attempting to single-handedly sustain a one-sided relationship, I would urge you to discontinue that relationship as soon as possible.

NINE FACETS OF RELATIONSHIP

Let's investigate nine different aspects of relationship and see how this Law of Mutual Benefit is either hindered or enhanced by takers and givers, respectively.

1. Value

When a giver pursues a relationship, he has one thing on his mind—he wants to *add value*. He is constantly searching for ways that he can esteem more, appreciate more, contribute more, and honor more. His focus is to bring greater weight to bear on the dreams and desires of his partner, and to continually add significance and worth to his partner's pursuits.

In sharp contrast, a taker is not looking to add, but rather, to *extract value* from the relationship. He might see that being associated with this particular person can potentially bring *him* more respect, honor, and recognition. His desire is to gain greater merit and support for his *own pursuits*, by attaching himself to what he perceives to be a prestigious, prominent, or influential individual. He disguises himself as a giver, one who is in your life to add value, but internally, you sense that the opposite is true.

The taker is continually searching for a more influential individual who will bring him greater benefits. The giver, on the other hand, creatively searches for ideas and ways to increase his value to the relationship.

The taker continually looks for connections whose influences surpass what his present circle of relationships offers. He is constantly scanning the horizon for "better contacts," and has no loyalty to the people he presently serves.

The giver is also conducting a search; however it's not for better contacts. It is for better ways of honoring and serving the ones to whom he has given his loyalty.

The giver goes to his boss and asks what it would take to become more valuable. She will go to her spouse to find out how she can better fulfill the role God gave her, in their marriage relationship. The giving son or daughter will go to his or her parents, to find out how to become more pleasing, more obedient, and how to fulfill every dream that the parents have for them. The taker does the exact opposite. *He is a user.* His self-indulgent attitude is an abomination.

NEVER ALLOW THE GIFTS THAT HAVE BEEN BESTOWED UPON YOU TO EVER ECLIPSE THE ONE WHO BESTOWED THEM.

My wife Linda is an incredible giver. She has given me the best years of her life. Linda loved me and cared for me when I was nothing. Linda will now get the best years of my life, in gratitude and in thankfulness, for having to put up with all the pressures of my life. Linda will always hold a voice in my life, even in my darkest hour.

When God puts people like Linda into your life, you keep them close to you. You don't just arbitrarily remove such voices because they no longer say the words that you want to hear.

Never allow the gifts that have been bestowed upon you to ever eclipse the one who bestowed them. I'll never forget the day that someone I once trusted sat across the desk from me and said, "The only reason that I wanted a relationship with you was because I knew what it would do for me." That statement revealed to me that all along, I had been in relationship with a taker and a user. Those words crushed me, and I am not sure I am completely done with them yet.

Givers energetically celebrate the people who have deposited goodness into them and have brought them to a place of success and favor. They celebrate their mentors in huge fashion, for this attitude of gratitude and humility keeps them from proudly thinking about the giftings in their own lives.

True givers never let the gifts they've received become more important to them than the giver of those gifts. Remember, the most inspired ideas for adding value in a relationship will spring from the fertile ground of a *grateful heart.*

2. Benefit

A giver is ever searching for what he can *contribute* to the relationship. However, the ever-present thought of a taker is, "What's in it for me?" He wants others to show an interest in *his* exploits and achievements. He searches for personal projects that would qualify for the support of influential givers.

As a son, I never ask for my fathers in the faith to be involved in anything that I do. I'm looking for a way to be involved with what *they* do. My question is, "What can I do for you?" not "What can you do for me?" It'll be that way until the day they die. *"What can I do for you?"* And I will do "as you wish."

The taker wants to own what the giver has earned through his seed. He will ask, "Why should God do all that for you? Don't you think you should share some of what God has given you?" This is his approach because he is a prodigal, who only wants to *own* what the giver has *earned.*

The giver wants to *know* what his mentor has *learned*, so that he can apply that wisdom in order to bring a contribution and a harvest back into the life of his mentor. He knows that the greatest truths in life do not come by learning something and walking way. The greatest truths come when *you choose to hang on,* even when circumstances aren't the way that you want them to be.

I grew up believing that whatever didn't serve me was unnecessary, and I should just get rid of it. I didn't recognize that I was an extremely needy person. I lived that way until I discovered that life isn't in having things that serve you. Abundant life is finding the pearl of great value, calling it precious, and *treating it as precious,* rather than taking it for granted or treating it with contempt and disrespect.

We must look for how we can *contribute* and bring benefit into the lives of others, instead of how we can *consume* and attempt to benefit ourselves. The reason that 20% of the members of an organization often have to do *everything* is because 80% of the people won't do *anything.* We must *stop consuming* and *start contributing,* for the mutual benefit of all.

3. Motivation

The focus of a giver is always turned outward. His thoughts are concentrated upon finding ways to position *others* to succeed. His motives are entirely altruistic and generous, having been birthed in a servant's heart.

Conversely, the thoughts and purposes of a taker are consistently selfish. He is motivated by greed and self-interest alone, showing apathy and indifference toward any situation or relationship that he feels will bring him no benefit. He believes that others should respond to *his* needs.

"Can't you see what I'm going through?"

I can't tell you how many times I've heard these words from the ungrateful takers in my life. Yet interestingly, when I walk into a room of grateful givers, they start crying, saying, "You cared for me when no one else did. You are so precious to me!"

To these givers I always respond, "I'll be precious to you until the day that you die. You just keep pressing. I will make up for all of the people that ever betrayed you. I'll wipe away all the tears and all the pain that people have brought to you."

My motivation is to make sure that those who have sown into my life receive a harvest from that precious seed. There *must* be reciprocity; there *must* be harvest from seeds sown.

Many times people want forgiveness, but they don't want to forgive. *They* want to be pardoned, but they want to continue to blame and point a finger at others. Let's say that you invested twenty years of sowing into a relationship. Don't you think that at some point you would get into the reaping phase? Part of the curse of the law is that people would have children, and someone else would enjoy them.

I will *not* allow myself to become a non-producing, barren son. I will continue to tune my heart to hear the whisperings of my fathers. I will listen—*really listen*— to what they *do not say,* as much as what they say. I will seek to understand *them,* not just their words. I will value the *relationship* more than the *results,* knowing that in focusing on the relationship, the results will come. I will *sow* compassion and kindness, because I realize how very much I need to *receive* compassion and kindness.

4. Rewards

A giver is not motivated by the recognition of men or temporal rewards. He does everything with his heart turned towards the eternal rewards that only heaven can bring. He is not concerned with self-preservation or self-protection, for he knows that as he takes care of others, God will take care of him.

A taker, however, is *driven* by the applause and approval of men. No matter how much he receives, it's never enough. In fact, a taker is oppressed by the fear of never having enough—never enough recognition, influence, respect, financial reward, or power. This incessant, nagging fear causes him to be a "user." Having no regard for the *people* in his relationships, he sees those associations as mere stepping-stones to get where he wants to go.

You can always spot people who pursue a relationship for what they can get out of it, because they are actively seeking others to solve their problems. Then, once their crisis is over, they disappear. The only time you ever hear from a taker is when he needs something!

Givers are generous, in relationship, because they trust God implicitly. They are willing to risk their entire future, based on that trust. Jesus was like that. When He was mocked and insulted, He did not retaliate—when He suffered, He did not threaten revenge, but instead He entrusted Himself to the Father, *"...who always judges fairly."*[1] He said, "God, I trust You."

Trust is a difficult subject for most people, due to the many times that others have hurt them and taken advantage of their trust. Before they even get to know people, they are already conditioned to believe that others are going to take advantage of them. And truthfully, most people distrust God for the same reason. But, how can I trust God with *my future,* if I will not trust Him with *my present?*

Ruth was an individual who trusted God so completely that she was willing to risk her entire future. When her husband died, she did not have to stay and take care of her mother-in-law, Naomi. In fact, her sister-in-law, Orpah gave Naomi a kiss and *then left her.* But we are told that Ruth *clave* unto Naomi. Orpah was a *kisser,* but Ruth was a *cleaver.*

There are a lot of people that will 'kiss' you, but Solomon tells us *"...the kisses of an enemy are deceitful."*[2] Beware of the people that are 'kissers' in your life. Kissers should always be willing to prove to you who they are. Are they going to *kiss and leave,* or are they going to *kiss and cleave?*

Ruth made the choice to cleave, saying these words, *"'Don't ask me to leave you and turn back. I will go wherever you go and live wherever you live. Your people will be my people, and your God will be my God. I will die where you die and will be buried there. May the Lord punish me severely if I allow anything but death to separate us!' So when Naomi saw that Ruth had made up her mind to go with her, she stopped urging her."*[3]

This is the choice that Ruth made. She chose an eternal reward, rather than a temporal reward; but in doing so, she also obtained a temporal reward! Her choice was to be a giver rather than a user.

Friend, you'll get more fulfillment from *committing* to believe the best about a challenging person, than having an *uncommitted* relationship with a wonderful person.

1. 1 Peter 2:23, *NLT*
2. Proverbs 27:6
3. Ruth 1:16-18, *NLT*

Every great man or woman is being pursued by *both* givers and users. In Chapter One we discussed Elijah and Elisha, and the exchange that happened between them at the end of Elijah's life.[4] God had spoken to Elijah and told him to go and anoint Elisha as being the prophet in his stead. In spite of the fact that there were other 'sons' of prophets who were following Elijah, Elisha was the only son who received Elijah's anointing. The other sons had *used* their relationship with Elijah only to become what *they* wanted to become. In the end, they were somewhat put back, disappointed, and resentful when Elisha received the reward of transparent relational intimacy. They didn't understand that *selfish motives are never rewarded.*

5. Protection

The evidence of love is protection. When a giver commits to a meaningful, loving relationship, he will do everything he can to protect the one he loves. This includes demonstrating that love through confrontation and correction, if necessary.

Often, the greatest threat to a person does not come from the outside of that person, but rather from *within*. As we've already discussed, the heart of man is very susceptible to being deceived. Believing and acting upon a deception is the way that many people open the door to loss in their lives. Unless we have cultivated relationships with people who love us enough to tell us the truth, it is quite likely that we will sabotage ourselves.

Jude, the brother of James, reminded his family that there is a time to forcefully speak the truth in love: *"But others save with fear, pulling them out of the fire..."*[5] If one were to do a study of the original Greek words used in this quote, it could be translated as follows:

> **Because of the alarmingly dangerous state that some people are in, I urge you to take immediate and fast-acting measures to see them delivered and rescued. And if they don't quickly respond, don't stop! You need to keep up your sense of urgency until you are convinced that they are rescued and snatched out of the fires of destruction. If you must, go all the way to grab them by the back of their necks and jerk them out of those flames...**[6]

4. See 2 Kings 2
5. Jude 1:23
6. Rick Renner, *Sparkling Gems from the Greek* (Tulsa, OK: Teach All Nations, 2003), p. 41-42.

A giver is not afraid to "face off" and forcefully speak the truth in love, if he must. Since he has truly *invested* himself into the relationship, he cares about his partner too much to remain silent and watch him be destroyed.

A taker, on the other hand, doesn't really care what happens to someone else, as long as it doesn't touch him. He will not risk the possible rejection of attempting to protect others from themselves. Not only does he refuse to "face off," but he gets highly offended and resentful when someone tries to lovingly correct him.

When a giver needs to be corrected, his response is, "Please forgive me, you never should have had to come to me. I should have straightened that out myself. I should have fixed that in my own heart and in my own life."

When a taker is corrected, his response is anger and a hardening of his heart. He refuses to be a self-corrector, so he ends up transferring the responsibility of the outcome of his life to the people who will love him enough to give him a chance to improve. But even when given the chance, he does not change. His response to instruction is one of distrust and resistance.

The proof of distrust is the requirement of an explanation. Only if you distrust me, will you require an explanation for my instruction. You'll ask, "Why? Why should I? That's not what I want to do. That's not my will." But if you trust me, you will embrace my loving admonition, no questions asked.

People find it hard to embrace correction because they don't want to face the truth. But remember, if I'm going to acknowledge you as someone who has the right to speak into my life, I also have to accept from you what I don't *want* to accept from you. I can't begin to pick and choose my correction, saying, "Well, now, that I like, but that? I don't like that." Takers only take correction temporarily; the giver is willing to receive instruction indefinitely.

As the relationship grows, you must advance beyond merely 'taking correction' to *eagerly receiving instruction*. You *want* to be instructed, because you don't want to displease again. It is wisdom to lay aside offense and resentment, and receive with meekness the words that are able to cause you to win.

It's necessary that you cultivate a tender heart. "*And be kind one to another, tenderhearted, forgiving one another...*"[7] I don't know many tenderhearted people. Now, I know some cowards who would like to tell you that they have tender hearts! But being tenderhearted means that people can easily touch your heart and cause you to do what is right. They can quickly get beyond your reasoning and appeal to your pure, soft heart, being confident that you will do what's right every time.

Become a protector. If you see a loved one in error, be willing to risk his or her rejection in order to tell him/her the truth.

6. Respect

A giver graciously extends respect to others, yet at the same time, requires of himself that he *earn* the respect of others. He understands that the more challenging are the problems that he conquers, the quicker he will command others' respect.

An unselfish, obedient giver is a person of *regard*. He regards others' interests ahead of his own. But a disregarding taker is inconsiderate of another man's time or value. Takers not only completely disregard their own assignments, but they also disregard *yours*, distracting you from the scheduled things that you must do.

It's really funny—the takers around me always expect me to change my schedule, just so they can fit in. They believe that the whole world revolves around them!

Conversely, a giver will do whatever it takes to accommodate his partner. He understands that man's most valuable commodity is *time*, and that to accommodate his partner's schedule is to actually give him the gift of time.

I remember the time that a person of authority asked me to be on his radio program with him. So, I took a day off work, called him on the phone, and said, "When would you like me to be at the radio station?"

He answered, "Well, we're not going to go today. We're going to go tomorrow."

"It's no problem, sir," I replied. "I'll see if I can get the day off."

"Well, I really would like you to be there," he said.

"Well, I'll be there, then." So I called my boss and said, "Boss, things didn't

7. Ephesians 4:32

happen for us today, but he said that he is going tomorrow. Any problem for me to take off tomorrow, as well?"

"No," he said. "That's fine; I guess if you're going to do some radio stuff, that's probably pretty important to you."

I agreed, "Well, yes sir, it is." So, I took off the second day. Now, two days and forty percent of my pay are gone.

I called him and said, "I got the day off—what time would you like me to be there?"

"Well," he responded. "I can't go today—I'll need to go tomorrow, and I'd like you to be there."

So I replied, "Yes, sir. I'll be there, sir." And I was.

But even with sixty percent of my pay gone, I want to honestly tell you—I never had a negative feeling. (And mind you, those were the days when Linda and I *couldn't* take a day off work—not a day, not an hour!)

So, on the third day, I went to the radio station, and as this gentleman and I were walking down a hallway, he turned to me said, "I'm not looking for a friend, you know."

"Sir," I respectfully acknowledged. "God didn't call me to be your friend. He called me to be your servant. I didn't come here to be your friend."

He did not know that I was a giver. I was looking to sow, not to take.

Once again, it is important for you to remember that the way that you treat any relationship, when you no longer need it, immediately reveals the motives that you had for it from the beginning. Time will reveal everything you need to know about every person.

7. Satisfaction

What satisfies and fulfills a taker, in relationship, is the opposite of what brings satisfaction to a giver. Real satisfaction rarely enters an ungrateful heart. For this reason, a taker can never truly taste the sweet joy of contentment and fulfillment. But, if you were to ask a taker what would bring him the most satisfaction and enjoyment, his answers would all be centered on his *getting*.

The taker wants what the giver has, and is most 'satisfied' when he thinks he's about to get it. The giver, by contrast, gains the most gratification and joy when *giving*. Nothing else in his life matches the pure pleasure, bliss, and fulfillment that he derives from being a giver!

I've often joked about needing to get my "giving fix" for the day, for it seems I am *addicted* to giving! If there were such a thing as "Givers Anonymous," I would have to attend the meetings, stand up in the front of the room, and say, "Hello. My name is Robb, and I'm a giver." But, truthfully, this is one addiction from which I *don't* want to be delivered!

Think about parental relationships (both natural and spiritual) for just a moment. A true son has no greater joy than when he is able to sow value into the life of his father. His heart is so full of gratitude that it overflows and becomes the creative impetus for finding new ways to express honor to his father. He feels privileged and humbled by the opportunity to serve a great man, and his humility opens new doors of intimacy.

Gratitude is the key that opens the door of tomorrow. Loss is the only thing that will grab the attention of the individual who is unthankful. I discovered that my future is linked to the level of gratitude that I show in my current relationships.

8. Purpose

When an individual operates from a posture of gratitude, he is continually calculating how he can *bless* others. He is acutely aware of how much he has been given, so he approaches all of life with a desire to give to others.

The antithesis to this grateful attitude is seen in the perspective of a taker. He is not thankful for what he has, but rather, is in a perpetual state of frustration and anger over what he doesn't have. He sees his glass as half empty instead of half full, and his mental energy is spent calculating how he can manipulate someone to get what he wants.

When in relationship with an influential giver, the taker believes that the giver should use his influence and friendships to enhance him. He wants to ride the giver's coattails to greatness. He selects public moments where associating with the mentor transfers credibility to him. He is always looking for an advantage. His plan is to *use* his relationship to gain inside knowledge, influence, respectability, and acceptance. Once he feels he has accomplished this objective, he will disparage the reputation of the giver and quickly exit the relationship.

The taker wants the mentor to teach him what he knows, so that he can take that knowledge and end the relationship. The giver wants to be warned of the things that he will need to know in order to avoid pitfalls, have success, and bring honor to his mentor.

I am a giver. This means that I will take care of my responsibilities. I don't need to be manipulated, maneuvered, or coerced into doing the right thing. I will do what principle tells me to do, independent of whom it benefits (because frankly, there are people whom I am called to honor, that I would prefer to kick in the shins!)

When you walk by principle, God may be the only one celebrating you. Even those who benefit from your integrity and honor will often be unappreciative. Don't be hurt, angered, or controlled by the responses that you get.

In the long run, getting the response you want depends on what you *sow* into a situation, not on how you *manipulate* a situation. For example, when I choose to live by Divine principle towards my wife, loving her sacrificially and unselfishly, her response to me is to reverence and respect me (to give me what I crave to have.)

Note: When working on developing your character in the arenas of giving, honoring, and sacrificially laying your life down for others, don't discount or disregard the benefits of walking it out with your family.

9. Personal Ethics

It is *acceptance of personal responsibility* in the areas of character and integrity that is the hallmark of a genuine giver. He is at all times mindful of his obedience and accountability *before God*, and this objective affects each and every relationship he enters. The people in his life become the beneficiaries of his commitment to honor.

I've learned that character is something that some people want *you* to have, so that *they don't have to.* Takers find it much easier to define your role than to walk in their own. They find it easier to identify the mistakes that you might be making than to admit to the wrong that they are doing. Just remember, most people who say they have a problem with you, actually have a problem with themselves. Usually, they are hoping that you will just change the way that you are; then they won't have to change at all.

Takers are not interested in doing the work of personal character development, because that would mean they would have to discipline themselves and deny their selfish desires. So, they lean much more heavily on *your* character than they do on their own. They want you to bear integrity and "carry" them, so that they can be irresponsible.

Solomon once said, *"Putting confidence in an unreliable person is like chewing with a toothache or walking on a broken foot."*[8] Relying on an irresponsible person to do the right thing is *very painful.* It's like chewing on an abscessed tooth! An irresponsible person will lean more on the reliability of *your* character, because he will not develop his own.

Takers can become so adept at relying on your generosity, that they will actually manipulate a situation to make you feel guilty about not giving to them! For example, most virtuous people accept that if they see a needy person, and they can help, they should. This is well and good if the person with the problem is of virtuous character. It becomes much more complicated if they are *professional takers.* These wolves in sheep's clothing know that you're "supposed to help them," and their hand is always out (not to give, but to take!) They have no hesitation over taking advantage of your generosity and defrauding you for as much as they can get.

What I would like to say to all professional takers is this—Divine principle does not say that anyone is *supposed to help you;* it says that *you're supposed to help someone.*

But now wait a minute, doesn't that mean the same thing?

No, it doesn't! Even if you are a person that gets helped, it can't be because you *manipulated* someone to help you. It's because *you helped someone else* that

---

8. Proverbs 25:19, *NLT*

you are helped. Remember, what you make happen for others, God makes happen for you.[9]

As givers we must take responsibility for our personal ethics. We must clothe ourselves with compassion, kindness, humility, gentleness, and consistency (patience). To clothe myself with something means that I can learn it. Even if I didn't get these traits when I was growing up, I can still learn how to be a tenderhearted, compassionate person. Just like articles of clothing, I can actually *take off* the negative influences that have run my life up until now, and I can *put on* traits of compassion.

You came into this world naked, and you will leave it the same way. You won't be taking anything with you. The only thing you have in this life that will extend beyond your death is your character. Develop strong moral integrity and dignity. Be a person who swears to his own hurt and will not change.[10] "Swearing to your own hurt" means that you give your word, and you keep your word, even when it hurts. You keep your commitments, pay your bills, and do what you say you're going to do.

You might say, "I don't like the way that they treated me." It doesn't matter how they treated you. You just shut your mouth and do what you're supposed to do *to please God.*

However, be cautious when dealing with a dishonorable individual. You really cannot keep your word to a dishonorable individual, because they don't believe in the strength and integrity of what you say anyway.

> INTEGRITY
> IS THE FOUNDATION UPON
> WHICH YOUR LIFE IS BUILT.

Dedicate yourself to a life of clear personal ethics. Go all the way with it. Don't compromise. Don't start listening to the voice that says, "You don't have to be such a stickler on principle." You must strive to do what is right, and not give up the principles that you vowed to build your life upon. Remember: *Integrity is the foundation upon which your life is built.*

It's funny to me when others believe more in my integrity than they believe

9. Murdock, *Dream Book*, p. 22. See Ephesians 6:8, *KJV*
10. See Psalm 15:4

in their own. They can trust that I'll do the right thing. They know that I will honor Divine principles, no matter what. I have vowed to live a pleasing life before God. As a result, those in relationship with me will be the beneficiaries of my walk with Him.

LIFE IS CHOICE, NOT CHANCE

Whether or not you see the Law of Mutual Benefit at work in your relationships will largely be a matter of *your choice.* You must choose whether you are going to be a giver or a taker, a sower or a prodigal. You must also choose with whom you are going to build relationships. *These important choices will determine the outcome of your life.*

Most people know the story of how Judas Iscariot betrayed Jesus. In fact, in modern culture, the term "Judas" has become synonymous with the word "traitor."

But Judas was more than a traitor. His betrayal of Jesus was not confined to one event at the end of their relationship. Judas was a betrayer *throughout the entire relationship.* Judas was a prodigal, constantly looking out for himself and calculating ways to *take*, in his relationship with Jesus.

When Mary expressed her profound gratitude toward Jesus by anointing His feet with expensive perfume, Judas chided her, saying, *"'That perfume was worth a small fortune. It should have been sold and the money given to the poor.' Not that he cared for the poor—he was a thief who was in charge of the disciples' funds, and he often took some for his own use."*[11]

A prodigal is a thief, an individual who takes what he can get out of any relationship he has. He rejects commitment, yet he expects to receive it. He continually wants to make withdrawals from the relationship without making any deposits into it. He greedily seeks the *benefits* of relationship, while refusing any of the *responsibilities.*

---

11. John 12:5-6, *NLT*

Jesus actually entrusted his moneybag to a thief. Now, I don't think that any of us in our right mind would entrust our money to a thief, do you? So what was that all about? Jesus was interested in Judas being able to turn it around. Judas was not *predestined* to be a betrayer—he had to make the *choice* to betray.

In trying to comprehend this fact, your mind might be saying, "Yes, but didn't God, in His foreknowledge know what Judas would do?" The answer is yes, but God doesn't use His foreknowledge to put things in place the way that He wants them. If God were going to do that, don't you think that He would have put things in order and taken care of this world a long time ago? God is not a taker—He will not take away the power of choice that He gave us so long ago.

MOTIVES

For every truth given to us by God, there is a counterfeit thrust upon us by the Liar. The differences between the two are often hard to distinguish, because many times they look and sound the same. But, you can *always* distinguish the difference by examining *the motives.* On the surface, the Law of Mutual Benefit may appear and sound like "you wash my back and I'll wash yours." In this counterfeit, productivity is based upon *mutual dishonesty.*

> EXCELLENT RELATIONSHIPS ARE DEFINED NOT BY WHAT I CAN REAP, BUT BY WHAT I CAN SOW.

Counterfeits are *always* based upon selfish motives. If your motive is to advance your own agenda by kissin' up to someone who can make it happen, then you are operating in the *counterfeit* principle of reciprocity. *It is the **motive** that makes all the difference.*

The true Law of Mutual Benefit springs from a pure, pristine motive of unselfishness. It comes from a heart whose primary objective is seeing the counterpart succeed. Its foundation is the unquestioned trust and confidence that "what I make happen for others, God will make happen for me."[12] Therefore, my focus is not upon myself and my agenda; my focus is upon others.

THE LAW OF MUTUAL BENEFIT

The quality of any relationship
is completely dependent upon the willingness of mutual pursuit.

→ **Never allow the gifts that have been bestowed upon you to ever eclipse the one who bestowed them.**

→ **Integrity is the foundation upon which your life is built.**

→ **Excellent relationships are defined not by what I can reap, but by what I can sow.**

---

12. Murdock, *Dream Book*, p. 22. See Ephesians 6:8, *KJV*

THE LAW OF
SACRIFICE

SACRIFICE IS THE ROAD TRAVELED
ON THE JOURNEY TO YOUR DIVINE DESTINY.

8

SACRIFICE IS THE ROAD TRAVELED
ON THE JOURNEY TO YOUR DIVINE DESTINY.

The greatest expression of a genuine *motive of giving* will be *self-sacrifice.* Sacrifice is as necessary to a relationship as pain is to building one's personal character. Sacrifice and pain are neither desirable nor enjoyable, but they are both unavoidable if we are to grow and have success, in life as well as in our relationships.

Building beneficial relationships involves *personal risk* and *personal cost*— but the prize of a positive, life-changing relationship far outweighs the price of personal sacrifice. Many people neglect the pursuit of significant people in their lives, in order to pursue *success.* However, the moment you sacrifice relationship to pursue success, you have just unknowingly sabotaged your success.

True success is only possible through the nurturing of wise relationships. Relationships are the keys that unlock the doors to a successful future. They are the strategically placed gateways to a new level of favor and productivity. But, it is impossible for this kind of success and advancement to just materialize and fall upon you like rain from heaven!

We live in a society that desires to "take its ease." People don't work for their employers or businesses anymore—they work for *the weekend,* when they can relax and take it easy! We have become the technologically savvy "microwave generation," expecting our needs and desires to be met instantly, effortlessly, and painlessly.

It's no surprise that people have the same expectations when it comes to their relationships. They do not understand that rich, meaningful relationships require an intense amount of thought, time, effort, attention, and commitment—or, in a word, *sacrifice.*

THE COST OF RELATIONSHIP

Successful relationships will cost you a significant price. You must be willing to pay that price if you desire to open the door to your future. The plans and purposes of God in your life have immeasurable and infinite value, and are worth the investment of your very life. If you were able to step into that destiny easily, without sacrifice or expense, you would esteem it too lightly and readily neglect, misuse, or lose it.

I never regret the sacrifice and cost of pursuing and maintaining relationships. In the end, God will recognize all of the deposits that I have made, and by using that seed, He will be able to do something with *my* life. In the next thirty-five years, if I become anything, it will not be because of the greatness that I possess—it will be because I was willing to bow my knee before others, as well as before God. Divine principle tells us that when we bow our knee, we will be exalted. It is when we choose the back seat at the feast, that we will be brought forward—*but not a moment sooner.*

Follow-through in any relationship is absolutely critical. Often, this requires you to deposit value into the relationship with great abandonment—usually with much more fervency than the one who is benefiting from your sacrifice. And so, *loneliness* becomes a constant companion.

When a person comes to greatness in his life, you'll find that he is frequently alone. Here are a few biblical examples:

* Jesus alone on the cross[1]
* Moses alone on Mt. Sinai [2]
* Joshua alone: *"Moses my servant is dead..."*[3]
* Gideon alone: *"Get up you mighty man of valor."*[4]
* Nehemiah alone before the king[5]
* Ruth alone in a country that wasn't her own[6]
* Esther alone as a Jewess in the palace of one who is just about to pass a decree that all Jews should be executed[7]

When you come to the place in your life where you are truly going to make a mark in history and in eternity, a tremendous amount of solitude will begin to accompany you. When you begin to make decisions toward excellence, don't think that a lot of people are going to clamor at your door, wanting to go with you; they won't. As a matter of fact, it will seem, for a time, that you are going down the wrong road. But, you've got to continue to travel down that road in order to become what God wants you to be.

The cost of nurturing an excellent relationship is constant and unremitting. It's in the daily choices of saying 'no' to yourself, and 'yes' to someone else. It's in meeting the demanding expectations that others unthinkingly or unspokenly place upon you. It's in looking after another man's interests, wealth, and welfare instead of your own. It's in losing your life, that you may find it, and in pursuing eternal rewards instead of temporal ones. The cost is dear—but so is the crown!

---

1. See Mark 15:34
2. See Exodus 19
3. See Joshua 1:1-2
4. See Judges 6:12
5. See Nehemiah 2
6. See Ruth 1:15-17
7. See Esther 5:1-2

THE VALUE OF RELATIONSHIP

Wisdom from heaven tells us that the greatest among us will be the servant of all.[8] Choosing servanthood doesn't mean that you're going to make sure that everyone in the room has a drink, or that everyone gets a plate when it's time to have something to eat. Choosing servanthood is actually *becoming what someone else needs at any particular moment, in order that they may achieve their purpose and goals.*

Any relationship that is worth pursuing is worth pursuing with abandonment. I found that my greatest input toward certain individuals was to pursue them with such abandon, and bless them so greatly as to cause them to lose focus of the people who had disappointed them. I could actually help them to focus on the *good things* that people would bring into their lives, instead of the bad. This shift in focus is important because greatness will never come out of individuals as long as their focus is on the unjust things that continue to happen to them.

> ANY RELATIONSHIP THAT IS WORTH PURSUING IS WORTH PURSUING WITH ABANDONMENT.

The value you place on anything is immediately revealed by the price you are willing to pay for it. I came to the realization that I greatly valued these relationships, because I was willing to give up my own pursuit of greatness in order to bring greatness to another. And, to this day, when I recognize that greatness is coming out of an individual, I tell him, "Your best years are ahead of you! And I'm here to multiply who you are and never bring you a day of grief."

> THE VALUE YOU PLACE ON ANYTHING IS IMMEDIATELY REVEALED BY THE PRICE YOU ARE WILLING TO PAY FOR IT.

I discovered that if I could actually bring out the best in others, they no longer had to work, strive, and push so hard

---

8. See Mark 10:42-44

for themselves. They could begin to *sow* instead of to protect themselves and hold on to what they had. They were now looking to see what they could do *in my life. Because they were now sowing, they could actually begin to truly reap.* This is the greatest value that I could ever bring to a person's life.

WILLING TO INVEST

Relationship requires investment. Investment means you are willing to take the risk to believe in someone *before you see a return.* You are willing to not only encourage them verbally, but also, as the old adage goes, to "put your money (your time, your energy, your favor, etc.) where your mouth is." My willingness to invest in wise relationships is proof that I desire a deeper relationship with God.

> MY WILLINGNESS TO INVEST IN WISE RELATIONSHIPS IS PROOF THAT I DESIRE A DEEPER RELATIONSHIP WITH GOD.

In previous chapters, we discussed Elisha's willingness to sacrifice his own life in order to invest himself into Elijah. It is important to note that Elisha had, first and foremost, invested his life into his commitment to serve God. Serving Elijah simply became the vehicle through which he could walk out that commitment. Elisha pursued his relationship to Elijah with such abandonment, and invested himself to such a degree, that he actually became cut off from himself.

As you sacrificially pour yourself into relationship, you come to the place where you almost lose yourself. You must learn how to live your life *without you—without your selfish ambitions.* (Remember, fleshly ambitions are like addictions. The more that you feed them, the less satisfied they are. Starve them and you are free!)

One of the greatest ways to get rid of your own problems is to solve someone else's. As you focus on taking care of someone else's interests, all of a sudden you'll look around and find that your problems are gone. That's one of the rewards of becoming a problem solver. Jesus said, "*...Sufficient unto the day is the evil there-of.*"[9] So, if you're solving someone else's challenges and problems, you've already got enough evil sufficient for your day and can't take any more evil. You have filled your quota!

LOVING PEOPLE BECAUSE YOU LOVE GOD

Loving individuals enough to stick with them and bring out the best in them can be challenging, at best. But if you determine to love God through them, (not necessarily because you like *them,*) then you can love, regardless of their actions.

If you do not have a strong relationship with God, this may be difficult for you to understand. For instance, you really don't work for your boss, but for God. It doesn't matter who is giving the orders; it only matters how you respond to them. Your response to the orders given by your superiors is proof of your private walk with God.

This principle applies not only to relationships with your superiors, but with all your relationships. You love your wife, not because she's always so lovable, but because you are head over heels in love with God. It really shouldn't matter how a person is treating you. You are accountable to God for the way you act. The proof of your commitment to God is displayed in your willingness to lay down what you want and to lovingly care for those to whom you are responsible.

The way that *you* choose to obey instruction or carry out your responsibilities has absolutely nothing to do with anyone else. For example, there was once a situation where Peter, after having just received some serious instruction from Jesus, turned around, pointed at John, and asked, "What about him?"

Jesus looked at Peter and replied, "Now, listen. Whatever I want someone else to do is *none of your business.* You just do what I'm telling *you* to do, and forget

---

9. Matthew 6:34, *KJV*

everyone else. (paraphrased)"[10] You do what *you're* supposed to do. Don't inspect other people to see if they're doing what they're supposed to do. *You just do what you're supposed to do.* Your obedience will be the practical proof that you truly love God. When I learned that, my life got tremendously easier.

Love is not something you *feel.* Love is something you *do.* You need to declare your love with your *actions,* as well as your words. Make decisions and choices not based upon what people want, but upon what God desires.

MAINTENANCE

All relationships need maintenance. Some require daily vigilance, in order to stay healthy, while others will require weekly or monthly attention. But, a relationship that is given *no* attention does not even qualify to be called a relationship. *A relationship that is not maintained is non-existent.*

> A RELATIONSHIP
> THAT IS NOT MAINTAINED
> IS NON-EXISTENT.

Occasionally I hear people say, "Gosh, I haven't talked to you for five years, and it's like we just talked yesterday. What a good friend you are!" This plainly cannot be possible, for you can't have a relationship with a person that you call a *friend,* if you haven't spoken to him for five years! Here's the reason why—*people lean and move toward the relationship that is meeting their most immediate need.*

An altruistic person might balk at the notion that the motive for relationship would be so 'self-serving.' But, if you honestly examine the ebb and flow of your own relationships over the years, you would have to admit that this observation is accurate. People gravitate towards those who are somehow meeting a need or solving a problem in their lives, whether it is emotional, intellectual, physical, or spiritual. They simply do not continue relationships that do not have some sort of

---

10. See John 21:20-23, author's paraphrase

a pay-off. People will sometimes even remain in what appears to be an abusive relationship, because somehow, someway, there is a core need that they believe is being met by the abuser.

If you do not invest time and energy to build up your relationships (marriage, friendships, mentors, and so forth), those relationships *will* degenerate. It doesn't matter who you are, or how excellent those relationships are at this moment. You could have the best marriage in the world, right now; but if you stop working on making your marriage better, your marriage will eventually die.

> WHAT YOU DO FIRST DETERMINES WHAT SOMEONE WILL DO NEXT, BECAUSE ANYTHING THAT IS DONE WILL CAUSE A RESPONSE.

An important principle to remember, when maintaining relationships, is The Law of Response: *What you do first determines what someone will do next, because anything that is done will cause a response.*

If you do something that is negative toward someone, it will bring out a negative response. If you do something that is positive, there will be a positive response. That response will not necessarily come from the person that you acted toward, but there will be someone who is watching that has the ability to reward you or to demote you for what you've done.

Therefore, if you want a positive response from someone you are pursuing, get out there and become the first one to do something beneficial in that person's life. What you do *first* will determine someone else's response. This principle works in every area of life. In fact, I live every relationship in my life based upon the Law of Response.

Understand this: You must keep every relationship *in front of you,* not just lackadaisically weave in and out of people's lives. No! You *purpose* to be the *creator, not the reactor* in every relationship, and that way you can determine how each and every relationship is going. Even in comparing the two words, *creator* and *reactor,* the only difference between them is the placement of the letter "c"— the positioning of the "see-er". The creator is the one who "*sees*" first and takes the initiative. The *reactor* simply responds to him.

That's exactly what God did for us. God, the Creator, made the first move. He *first* loved us.[11] And do you realize that ever since we came face to face with that love, that you and I have been doing everything in our power to love Him back! Ever since we learned of His Unspeakable Gift,[12] we have attempted to do everything we could to pay Him back, (even though we know we cannot possibly do so.) We love God because He *first* loved us.

But I see people who refuse to invest *anything* in others, because "they just don't seem to like me." That's like looking at the fire and saying, "Would you give me some heat, and then I'll give you some wood." Um, *first* you put in the wood, *and then* the wood actually burns to give you the warmth you desire! Understand that every relationship is just like that; *first* you sow into a relationship, *and then* that relationship becomes to you what you desire it to be.

I search everyday to become what's needed in the lives of others, not to sit back and say, "Bless God, this is just the way I am." Whatever I need to be in any relationship is what I'm going to become; I just need to know what that is. I am never going to try to make anybody line up with what I want. I am going to line up with what other people need, because that gives me my right to relate.

Friend, you don't know what's in front of you. You do not know what risks are out there or what lies in your future. But, if you keep sowing into other people's lives, then even when destruction comes at you, you've got reaping waiting to come in, and no matter what, you'll get through that tough time.[13] And that's when you begin to understand how crucial relationships are.

Now, this kind of protection and favor can happen for anyone. You don't have to do anything except take inventory of your seed and be willing to sow it. Maybe you can't do anything but shine someone's shoes, or be a person who is willing to listen when someone needs a listener. Whatever kind of seed that you have, just begin to sow it! Start asking yourself, "How can I love this person? How can I say the right things to them? Lord, give me the words that will actually cause them to be promoted in life. Do something through me, God; I have *got* to *sow* now, not

11. See 1 John 4:19
12. See 2 Corinthians 9:15, *KJV*
13. See Ecclesiastes 11:2

reap! Teach me how to apply the Law of Sacrifice."

What I learned was that I could bring value, *no matter where I started.* God has put *something* in my hand with which I can create my future, no matter how small or insignificant that seed appears to be. You must see that you don't need anything but seed, in order for God to create a future for you. Learn to be a sower because God will *only supply seed to the sower.*[14]

So, the Law of Response shows me that whatever I deposit into the life of another will determine how that individual will respond back to me. How we face off with anything in life will ultimately dictate how it comes back at us. Rather than being reactors, we must *take the initiative* and *set the tone* in every situation, no matter how bad.

Let's say that things get off track, and a relationship goes bad. What does Divine principle instruct us to do? Try to explain it to them so that they understand? No! *"Bless those who curse you..."*[15] In other words, don't *react* to what they have done but instead, jump-start the Law of Response all over again. Whenever you're thrown into the *reacting* side of a situation, you begin to lose, because you have to respond to people. So, Wisdom tells you to turn it around and get on the *creating* side of the situation. When you get on the creating side, your life changes.

> THE PURSUIT OF EXCELLENCE CAN ONLY BE PROVEN BY THE ATTITUDE WITH WHICH YOU FACE THE GIANT NAMED "MAINTENANCE."

The pursuit of excellence can only be proven by the attitude with which you face the giant named "Maintenance." Although maintenance may seem like a boring, needless distraction, every relationship you have rests heavily on your ability to give it the attention it requires. Maintenance is probably the most necessary, yet most neglected aspect of relationship.

14. See 2 Corinthians 9:10
15. Luke 6:28

ENEMIES OF SACRIFICE

Let's examine two factors that stifle and thwart the Law of Sacrifice in our lives:

1. Comfort

One of the primary reasons that people neglect to maintain their relationships is that they want to pursue *comfort*. They become familiar and comfortable with the other person, and they allow that familiarity to breed neglect, lassitude, and indifference. They begin to *disregard* another, to take him or her for granted, and to take undue liberties.

The definition of *regard* is *respect coupled with affection*. We must *regard* the individuals in each of our relationships. We must continue to take notice of them, give them special attention, strive to please them, and highly value them in practical ways. Affection and appreciation need to be frequently and liberally expressed.

Disregard, on the other hand, means *to ignore or pay no attention to someone, or to treat someone with a lack of respect*. If we are not watchful and diligent, **comfort** in relationship can lead to disregard. What was once precious now seems ordinary and unimportant. What was once treated with respect is now treated rudely. Responsibilities that were once given meticulous and prompt attention are now handled carelessly and sluggishly.

Do not look for comfort in relationships. Prolonged seasons of comfort produce *no positive change*. In the heating and cooling business, "comfort" is defined as the ability to go from one environment to another environment without feeling any change. Friend, this is *not* what you are looking for in your relationships!

No change means no growth. And no growth means certain death! If an organism is alive, it is in a constant state of fluctuation, change, and growth. Your relationships are the same way. Even if you've been married to the same person for fifty years, you must make sure that your relationship continues to grow and blossom.

Another reason that you must discard the idea of 'comfort' in relationship is that the *future bearers* in your life will cause you to be *anything but comfortable! Yesterday people* usually want to keep things predictable, mediocre, and, well...*comfortable.* But you must avoid mediocrity as if it were the plague, for it can kill you just as quickly. You need to pursue the people of *tomorrow* in your life, and refuse to settle or get comfortable. You must be willing to sacrifice your bed of ease and *choose the discomfort* of relationships that press you, prod you, and push you into your future. Sacrifice, discomfort, and risk are all *a choice.*

"I'm sorry," you may say. "I've already taken the risk of investing myself into people, and I've really been burned. I just don't know if I can take that risk again."

I understand your reluctance, for I've said those words myself. But I have made the decision to forsake comfort and to continue to believe—not for the sake of those who have abused my relationships with them, but for the people who have not. I don't want the people who have stayed faithful to me to pay the price for the people who have not.

When you have been hurt by relationships in the past, that hurt and that anger will come to you and talk to you. It will try to convince you to shrink back into a comfortable, protective shell and never again open yourself up to another human being. So, the *first* risk, the *first* discomfort, and the *first* sacrifice for a person who has been hurt is to purge himself. He must come to a place where he *chooses* forgiveness and rids himself of the anger, the bitterness, and the fear of vulnerability.

Those who have stuck with you should not be made to continually wade through the muck of your resentment. They should not have to pay the price of your anger and fear. Those who have faithfully loved you should not have to struggle to reach you and get you to open up to them. *You must choose* to no longer allow the anger and bitterness of the past to exert power over your life, your relationships, and your future.

Choose the discomfort of humility, for the pain of humiliation is much greater. Make the *sacrifice* necessary to be a *self-corrector,* before others are forced to bring correction to you. Remember, real change is *chosen change.*

I once heard a rather funny story of a man and his young son who were standing in a church service together, and it came time to sit down. So, the father sat down, but the son remained standing.

"Sit down!" the father whispered to his son.

The boy folded his arms across his chest and replied, "Nope."

Again, the father said, "Sit down, everybody's looking at you!"

And again, the son replied, "Nope."

At this point, the father grabbed him by the seat of his pants, yanked him down and said, "There! Now, you're sitting down!"

The boy's indignant response was, "I may be sitting down on the outside, but I'm standing up on the inside!"

Choose to make the changes yourself, before anyone else has to prompt you; otherwise, you'll still be "standing up" on the inside, when corrected, and making everyone around you pay the price of your bitterness and pain. Choose to *reject the comfort* of mediocrity, familiarity, and self-protection. *Embrace the discomfort* of excellence, honor, and vulnerability, and your life will dramatically improve.

2. Convenience

An accomplice to the trap of comfort is the snare of convenience. In order to achieve excellence in relationships, we must discard the idea of convenience, because excellence in relationship has *nothing* to do with convenience. The reason that people live conveniently in relationship is because convenience lives with mediocrity.

Average people are convenient. Common, normal, and ordinary people are convenient. But exceptional, rare, notable people will *never* be convenient. The exceptional people in my life require my pressing in, traveling the earth, and becoming a 'junior' in relationship, whereas respectfully, I don't have to be a junior in any relationship. I could establish myself in my own abilities, but I refuse to do so. I recognize that if God is going to promote me, I can never do it on my own—other relationships have to promote me.

Convenience implies minimal output of thought and energy, and a resulting inferior product. Convenience is the opposite of sacrifice, dictating that I function only within the confines of my own preference, availability, ease, or enjoyment. The only price that convenience is willing to pay is the price to remain comfortable and undisturbed. But the Law of Sacrifice compels me to forsake convenience and to pay whatever price is necessary to push into my future and be a problem solver, rather than a problem.

One of the things that I'm learning and attempting to master is paying the price to answer a need *promptly* and get a job done *quickly, even before it has been spoken.* If something is in the power of my hand to do, my goal is to not withhold that good from those to whom it is due, but to do it without delay.[16] I realize that if I wait until it is *convenient* to do something I need to do for *you,* that maybe you will wait to do what you need to do for someone else. So, I don't give myself the 'luxury' of saying, "I'll take care of that tomorrow," or "I'll take care of that later on." No, I know there is something else for me to take care of tomorrow!

When I am willing to sacrifice my convenience, my time, and my resources to sow my seed into a relationship, I will, in time, reap a harvest, no matter what.

I might not receive back from the same individual all the good things that I brought into his life, but I *will* receive it back somewhere, somehow, someday, from someplace. It will come back to me. It is a perversion of the Divine to fail to reap what you have sown. In fact, it is impossible.

> YOUR HARVEST IS DETERMINED BY WHAT YOU SOW, NOT DECIDED BY WHAT YOU DESIRE.

The word *seed* means *beginning.* Every seed has a future, and no matter what you sow, God said that seed would bring forth fruit, either positive or negative. The Apostle Paul told the Galatians, *"Don't be misled. Remember that you can't ignore God and get away with it. You will always reap what you sow!"*[17] So, once again, you may not necessarily reap *where* you sow, but you will, *without fail,* reap *what* you've sown. God will make sure of it! It is your responsibility to recognize that

---

16. See Proverbs 3:27
17. Galatians 6:7, *NLT*

convenience is an enemy to your seed and to your future.

What is convenient costs me nothing. I will not give to my God or to my friends, love or attention that costs me nothing. To do so would be the highest form of dishonor imaginable.

When we embrace the Law of Sacrifice, we must forsake the notion of comfort or convenience. Only when we make the decision to discard convenience in our relationships, will we begin to discover God's reasons for them.

SACRIFICE THROUGH COMPASSION

Loving someone all the time does not always *feel good*. Sometimes you have to love a person when, at that particular moment, they're being quite unlovely. That takes compassion.

What does it mean to be a compassionate individual? People don't mind receiving compassion from others, but they don't like to give it because compassion, at times, can look like weakness. Friend, *compassion is not weakness; compassion is the proof of confident strength.* Only an individual with great strength of character will put aside his own needs and interests, to compassionately reach out to another human being and help him carry his burden.

There's a difference between a person who is *passionate* and a person who is *compassionate*. There are many passionate individuals, especially those who are enthusiastic about their personal "pet projects." But, to know a compassionate person is a privilege. To be a compassionate person is to become a rare individual, with an unrelenting pursuit to right every wrong that you see. A compassionate individual wants to be an answer in arenas where most people don't even know there's a question.

Compassion is an attitude of care and concern grounded in pity and sympathy towards others. It's coming to a place where I'm willing to suffer with others.

I'm willing to be pained by the distresses that they are going through, and to feel the very same anguish that they feel. Compassion is a sensation of sorrow that rises up when it sees the adversities or misfortunes of another. You actually become angry over the torment that another person has to endure, and you are willing to throw the ashes in the air with him and mean it from your heart.

Compassion is a mixed emotion; it's a compound of love and sorrow. The opposite of compassion is indifference—"I don't care what you're going through, because I don't have to deal with it. I've got my own pain to deal with." But, a person of compassion is willing to put his shoulder under the burden and pain of another and lift it off his back. To demonstrate such empathy and to sacrifice oneself to this degree is not easy; but it is a privilege that is inexpressibly fulfilling.

SACRIFICE THROUGH LONG-SUFFERING

One of the greatest expressions of sacrifice in a covenant relationship is the willingness to embrace *long-suffering*.[18] The term long-suffering comes from the Greek word *makrothumia*,[19] and gives us the picture of macaroni or taffy that you can pull and pull and pull and *pull*, and it just keeps stretching, and tolerating, and enduring, and continuing, and bearing, and remaining, and acting like it will *never break!* This is the type of sacrificial investment that genuine love will demonstrate.

My long-suffering will cause me to believe the best about people who are not yet demonstrating their best behavior. "This is what I am believing about them. This is what I'm standing for. This is what I want inside their life." I can continue this way *until it begins to affect another person.* The minute that their evil or weakness begins to affect, deceive, or steal from someone who is good, I can no longer extend *makrothumia.* They must be allowed to eat the bitter fruit of the path that they have chosen, because true love must sometimes be tough love.

Whether it is through compassion, long-suffering, or tough confrontation,

---

18. See 2 Timothy 4:2, *KJV*
19. James Strong, *The New Strong's Exhaustive Concordance of the Bible/Dictionary of the Greek Testament* (Nashville, TN: Thomas Nelson Publishers, 1990) p. 634/46.

laying down your life for someone can be expressed in countless ways. Laying down your life can mean (but is not limited to) literally dying to save another's life. Laying down your life can also be something you do day in and day out, in the innumerable choices of life. When you deprive yourself of sleep to care for your child, you are laying down your life. When you work long and hard to provide for your family, you are laying down your life. Any time you unselfishly deny your own needs, comfort, convenience, or desires in order to benefit another person, you are laying down your life and picking up the mantle of sacrifice.

WHAT YOU SHOULD NEVER SACRIFICE

In speaking of the Law of Sacrifice, we must understand that there are elements that we must be prepared to sacrifice (comfort, convenience, time, resources), as well as elements that we must *never* sacrifice. *We must never sacrifice integrity, character, or principle for the sake of relationship!*

Pay the price to be compassionate, but don't sacrifice principle to achieve this most noble of goals! Be willing to feel what people go through and to understand their plight, but never compromise truth.

> TO ENJOY LIFE WE MUST ALWAYS PRIZE PRINCIPLE ABOVE RELATIONSHIP.

To enjoy life we must always prize principle above relationship. If you stick with principle, you'll still be on the road many years after the self-proclaimed "VIP's" are dead and gone.

David declares:

> Blessed is the man who fears the LORD, who delights greatly in His commandments. His descendants will be mighty on earth; the generation of the upright will be blessed. Wealth and riches will be in his house, and his righteousness endures forever.[20]

---

20. Psalm 112:1-3

PASSING THE TESTS

Before there can ever be a promotion, there must always be a test. Before you are ever promoted to the next grade, you've got to go through finals. There isn't anyone who can escape this process. The same principle is true in relationships. You are never promoted in your relationships, until you pass the tests of your present level.

Unfortunately, there are those who have built a doctrine that says we don't need to go through testing. We are actually able to hear the TV programs and purchase the tape series that teach us that we don't have to go through the wilderness. But you are going to go through the wilderness. That is one trip that is *not an elective.* You're going! The wilderness is one place that each one of us has to experience.

It is the wilderness that will tell you whether you are a tree that has only leaves on it, or whether you are a tree that has fruit on it. Not only that, but when you are fruitful, you will be pruned. My thoughts are, "If I've got a fruit tree that's producing some fruit, let's leave that one alone, because he looks like he's doing okay." But, no, if you are making it, the first thing that will happen to you is you will be hacked in half. Why? *So you can produce more fruit.*

That's the reason that sometimes, you begin to see a chasm forming between individuals. People who were once close now seem to be growing apart. Usually it's because one person has gone into the wilderness, has been pruned, has passed his tests, and has advanced, while the other person has not.

So you have to realize that when you see people going through circumstances that are challenging for them, they are being tested. Their test is not with you or another person; *their test is with themselves.* It is their character and their integrity that is being tested. You can help them to prepare for their test, but you cannot pass the test for them—only *they* can pass their test.

THREE INESCAPABLE TESTS OF SACRIFICE

1. The Test of Character

Character is the fruit of submission. The fruit of character is moral strength, and the affect of moral strength is promotion. Character is not built when you are asked to do things you *want* to do. Character will only come to your life, in relationship, by doing things you *do not want* to do.

We can see an example of how character is built, by looking at the story of Joseph, in the book of Genesis. Joseph was given two visions. In the first vision, all of his brothers' sheaves bowed down to Joseph's sheave. In his second vision, not only did his brothers' sheaves bow down, but his father's did, as well.

It's great when God gives you a vision for your future. But, Joseph made a mistake. He talked about it. As a result, his brothers sold him into slavery, and he was sent to Egypt. There are times when you've just got to shut your mouth, and not talk about the workings of God in your life! In speaking about this situation, the psalmist says, *"There in prison, they bruised his feet with fetters and placed his neck in an iron collar. Until the time came to fulfill his word, the Lord tested Joseph's character."*[21] Another version says, until the time that his vision came to pass, the word of the Lord tested Joseph.

When I saw this, I thought about my own character and compromises. I came to this conclusion: the tests that I face today are insignificant compared to where I am going. The tests that some of my relationships are presently facing are nothing compared to where God wants to take those relationships. But until the fullness of those relationships comes to pass, my character will be tested to see if I'm willing to forsake selfishness in my life, and enter into The Law of Sacrifice.

2. The Test of Integrity

Some of the hardest tests and most sacrificial moments occur when I must confront and correct others. Confrontation is one of my least enjoyable activities. I'll do anything to avoid confrontation—anything, that is, *except* compromise

21. Psalm 105:18-19, *NLT*

integrity and principle! Remember: *Compromise is the willingness to accept what you don't believe, because you are unwilling to stand for what you do.*

Integrity is more important to me than any relationship. So, no matter how difficult it may be, if I see a trespass that must be addressed, I will stand for what I know is true.

I will *never* discard an individual. I've seen the ruthless pain of treating someone with this kind of disrespect and contempt, and I will never, ever take part in causing such pain. So, rather than discard a person, I must face off with him.

The choice to confront cannot be based on whether or not you like a person. Sometimes I have to sit certain people down to talk about their wrong. The reason I talk to them about it is because I *do* like them. If I didn't like them, I would just ignore the whole situation and let them go to their consequences.

> COMPROMISE IS THE WILLINGNESS TO ACCEPT WHAT YOU DON'T BELIEVE, BECAUSE YOU ARE UNWILLING TO STAND FOR WHAT YOU DO.

It's not fun or comfortable to talk to a friend about his trespasses and unprincipled behavior. But these are the moments in relationship when character is tested. These are the times when you must value the integrity of your relationship so much, that you cannot remain silent. You must value your friend enough to forsake comfort and convenience, risk rejection, and speak the truth in love.

God always puts the responsibility of the hard decisions upon the ones who will be the kindest. His motive is restoration; so He's looking for someone who will stand firm and immovable in principle and truth, yet speak that truth with kindness and love.

Concerning those who would not listen to wisdom, Solomon once said, *"That is why they must eat the bitter fruit of living their own way. They must experience the full terror of the path they have chosen."*[22] Now you have to understand, a path is not a destination. They are not yet at the destination; they are only in the process of walking down an unwise path. He said they must eat the bitter fruit of

---

22. Proverbs 1:31, *NLT*

the *path* that they have chosen. Why? Because God loves them so much, he's trying to stop them from having to experience the destructive destination at the end of the path; and you and I are His instruments of change.

3. The Test of Release

Sometimes, the greatest test of all comes when the one you love refuses to turn from his recalcitrant ways. When this happens, "sacrifice" means taking your hands off the situation and letting him make his choices. "Laying down your life" means enduring the agony of watching him face the consequences of those choices.

Consequences are the chosen experiences of those who have elected to walk their own way. Solomon once said, *"He who is often rebuked, and hardens his neck, will suddenly be destroyed, and that without remedy."*[23] We make a grand mistake when we attempt to stop Divine consequences from working in people's lives.

I understand that you care for them and don't want to see them going through pain, so you attempt to stop it. But you are not helping the person at all! Sometimes true love means you must get out of the way, and let them eat the fruit of their disobedience. The writer of Hebrews says, *"Anyone who is not chastised is not a son, but a bastard."*[24]

> CONSEQUENCES ARE THE CHOSEN EXPERIENCES OF THOSE WHO HAVE ELECTED TO WALK THEIR OWN WAY.

You have to understand that there is a difference between helping a person who is down and attempting to circumvent the hand of God in a person's life. I cannot stop consequences from coming to you. I must allow you to experience the reaping caused by the sowing you have chosen to do. I cannot stop those consequences, without your repentance. If you repent, then I can help you weather the storm. However, without repentance, it is important to let you walk it out. Why? Because if I get you off the hook today, then next week or two weeks from now, you are probably going to be in the same jam all over again!

How many times have you met someone that you *knew* you would have to fix? You got into relationship with them, and you needed to pull them out of

23. Proverbs 29:1
24. Hebrews 12:8, *KJV*, author's paraphrase

something that they were dealing with. You rescued them out of that mess only to find out that two months later they were in the same mess again.

We attempt to erase the reaping that is coming to people's lives, as a result of their unwise sowing. That is *not* love, and that is *not* laying your life down for them. *Sometimes the Law of Sacrifice calls us to allow our loved ones to experience the pain of consequence.* This may actually be the deepest and most heart-wrenching sacrifice of all.

THE PRIZE IS WORTH THE PRICE

The price of successful relationships can, at times, seem exorbitant and impossible to satisfy. But, we must remember that *love* is the one debt in our lives that can *never* be stamped "PAID IN FULL." The Law of Sacrifice invokes us to throw off every vestige of selfishness, and ungrudgingly lay down our lives in order to see another person *win*. And when the seed and sacrifice of your life begins to produce a mighty generation of overcomers and world-changers, then you'll know that the prize was definitely worth the price!

THE LAW OF SACRIFICE

Sacrifice is the road traveled
on the journey to your Divine destiny.

→ Any relationship that is worth pursuing is worth pursuing with abandonment.

→ The value you place on anything is immediately revealed by the price you are willing to pay for it.

→ My willingness to invest in wise relationships is proof that I desire a deeper relationship with God.

→ A relationship that is not maintained is non-existent.

→ What you do first determines what someone else will do next, because anything that is done will cause a response.

→ The pursuit of excellence can only be proven by the attitude with which you face the giant named "Maintenance."

→ Your harvest is determined by what you sow, not decided by what you desire.

→ To enjoy life we must always prize principle above relationship.

→ Compromise is the willingness to accept what you don't believe, because you are unwilling to stand for what you do.

→ Consequences are the chosen experiences of those who have elected to walk their own way.

→ The prize is worth the price.

THE LAW OF
SYNERGY

ONE CAN CHASE A THOUSAND,
BUT TWO WILL PUT TEN THOUSAND TO FLIGHT!

9

ONE CAN CHASE A THOUSAND,

BUT TWO WILL PUT TEN THOUSAND TO FLIGHT!

When you sacrificially sow the seed of your life into the right people, you step into a realm of production, promotion, and provision that would be unavailable to you if you attempted to pursue success on your own. Within *key relationships*, there resides an immeasurable amount of accelerative energy just waiting to be harnessed. The explosive momentum for increase that is produced when this energy is tapped is called *synergy*.

Two people can accomplish more than twice as much as one; they get a better return for their labor. If one person falls, the other can reach out and help. But people who are alone when they fall are in real trouble. And on a cold night, two under the same blanket can gain warmth from each other. But how can one be warm alone? A person standing alone can be attacked and defeated, but two can stand back-to-back and conquer. Three are even better, for a triple-braided cord is not easily broken.[1]

---

1. Ecclesiastes 4:9-12, *NLT*

These are the words of King Solomon, a man who many believe to be one of the wisest men who ever lived. His very first statement reveals that relationships do not merely *add* to our lives—*they multiply our lives.*

THE MULTIPLYING POWER OF RELATIONSHIP

God designed men and women, boys and girls for interdependence and multiplication. The human heart is a bed of rich, fertile soil, just waiting to receive the seeds of influence. Those seeds of influence are planted in our hearts by *our relationships*, and they *will* produce a crop that will manifest in our characters and in the outcome of our lives. It is a process that we can neither inhibit nor stop.

The very nature of influence is to bring multiplication.[2] Bad relationships will plant seeds of destructive influence, and the result will be a crop of bad outcomes and destruction in a person's life. By contrast, relationships with wise, honorable people will sow the seeds of wisdom and integrity into an individual's heart, producing a multiplication and harvest of wisdom, honor, favor, promotion, and blessing in that individual's life.

A human heart _will_, without question or doubt, multiply and produce whatever seeds of influence it receives. We cannot prevent the seeds from producing. However, what we *can and must do is choose,* on purpose, which seeds of influence are planted within our hearts. The only way to accomplish this is to be extremely selective in choosing our relationships.

---

2. John C. Maxwell, *Relationships 101-What Every Leader Needs To Know* (Nashville, TN: Thomas Nelson Publishers, 2003), p. 18.

ARENAS OF SYNERGY

The above quote by King Solomon speaks of three crucial arenas where the synergy of relationships will determine the outcome of our lives:

* **Protection**—*"If one person falls, the other can reach out and help. But people who are alone when they fall are in real trouble."* There is great safety and protection in surrounding yourself with wise counsel.[3] Because a mentor has gone down the road ahead of you, his guidance and direction are invaluable in avoiding decisions and situations that could destroy your future. The protective insulation that envelops your life is immensely increased by judicious relationships. Without these relationships, you are exposed and vulnerable to your own ignorance, as well as to the malicious deception of others.

* **Provision and Production**—*"And on a cold night, two under the same blanket can gain warmth from each other. But how can one be warm alone?"* Again, a key to seeing increase in your life is refusing to isolate yourself, but instead, joining forces with other productive, loyal people. The producing power of two people who are committed to each other and to a common cause will result in *more than the sum* of what these two would have produced alone. The unity of their hearts and the partnership of their perseverance generate a synergistic explosion that supernaturally accelerates progress and compounds provision.

* **Prevailing Power and Promotion**—*"A person standing alone can be attacked and defeated, but two can stand back-to-back and conquer."* Winning does not happen alone. If you are a successful person, you know that you did not get that way by yourself. Moses, the lawgiver, recognized the synergistic power of relationship when he said, *"One person can put a thousand to flight, and two can put ten thousand."*[4] You will multiply your winning power *ten times* when you can learn to submit yourself to one other person! Favor, promotion, and success burgeon within Godly relationships.

---

3. See Proverbs 11:14
4. Deuteronomy 32:30, author's paraphrase

CREATED FOR INTERDEPENDENCE

We have been designed for *interdependence*. We've been created to multiply within relationship, and what we allow inside our relationships *will* multiply, whether good or bad. But so often, because we don't want to face off with people who bring compromise into our lives, we allow destructive influences to remain, not realizing that these relationships are breeding poisonous toxins that are designed to damage our lives beyond repair.

Friend, whether you realize it or not, your integrity, character, and obedience are constantly being tested. Are you going to do what is right in your relationships? Or, are you going to do what you want? Are you going to do what is convenient and easy for you, or are you going to do what is inconvenient but necessary for you to do? You will either pass or fail the test. If you pass today's test, you will then enter upon another one. Each and every relationship that comes to our lives draws us into the law of sowing and reaping, so that in time we will reap those things that we have sown, whether positive or negative.

The Law of Sowing and Reaping is an immutable law of the universe, just like the Law of Gravity. *"As long as the earth remains, seedtime and harvest, summer and winter, cold and heat, and day and night will never stop."*[5] This is a law that even God cannot change in your life. It is forever established, and cannot be broken or overturned. In the same way that you have learned to work with the Law of Gravity, and use it to your advantage, you must learn to use the Law of Sowing and Reaping within your relationships, to multiply blessing and success into your life and the lives of others.

Let's talk about the spiritual applications of this principle for a moment. Do you know that both God and Satan *want to draw you into the Law of Sowing and Reaping, so that you can reap off of the things that you sow?* God believes in you so much that he expects that you will make right choices concerning your relationships, and reap the benefits of those right choices. The devil believes he can

5. Genesis 8:22, author's paraphrase

easily deceive you, just like he deceived Adam—so he is attempting to draw you into making harmful choices. Then, as you reap destruction off of the negative associations that you have allowed in your life, he will actually convince you to point your finger at God and accuse Him of not coming through for you! Satan will just sit back and laugh, as you blame *God* for your failure to sow the right seed into the right people. Solomon alluded to this when he wrote, *"People ruin their lives by their own foolishness and then are angry at the Lord."*[6]

Every moment of every day, your life is being tested. From the positive aspect, God is testing you *to promote your life.* From the negative aspect, the devil is attempting *to destroy your life.* If you make right choices, your character and your relationships will bring to pass the good things that God has ordained for you. All that you need to do is believe it and *act like you believe it;* then your life will be propelled into greatness.

God has an amazing future planned for you. How long are you willing to resist the negative influences in your life? As long as you are willing to stand (a defensive move) and withstand (an offensive move), the door to promotion remains open to you. Promotion and favor will be multiplied back to you as you refuse to compromise or give up principle, in your relationships. However, the multiplied influence of *negative synergy* will follow a person who continually shrinks back from taking a stand for what he knows to be right. Let's discuss this concept further.

NEGATIVE SYNERGY: MULTIPLICATION FOR THE WORSE

The Apostle Paul was referring to *negative synergy* when he said, *"I'm concerned about when you come together because, I know that some of you are not making one another better, but you are actually making one another worse."*[7] Many

---

6. Proverbs 19:3, *NLT*
7. 1 Corinthians 11:17, author's paraphrase

of us have had relationships in which spending time with people did not improve our lives, but rather, made them worse. Your relationships must make you *better*.

> IN ORDER TO HAVE A
> RELATIONSHIP WITH ONE,
> YOU JUST MAY HAVE TO
> DISCONNECT FROM ANOTHER.

If a relationship does not make you better, it's not meant for you.

People are either *demotions* or *promotions* for you. There is always someone sent to your life to cause you to *lose*. These are people whom you cannot afford to be around. You love them, you care for them, you want to spend time with them, yet, at the same time, you cannot afford to be with them; you realize that if you do, you'll become just like them. These people are your "yesterday people," and unless you disconnect from them, they will hold you back from your "future bearers."

Many people do not enter into better relationships, because they are unwilling to disconnect from previous relationships. They don't want yesterday's people to leave their lives. Many individuals think that they can have tomorrow's people along with yesterday's people; but God will not allow you to have mingled seed in your life. He will never give us tomorrow's relationships until we're willing to let go of yesterday's. Remember: *When you are looking for your future, you will never find it in your past.*

We see an example of Jesus operating in this principle when he disconnected

> WHEN YOU ARE
> LOOKING FOR YOUR FUTURE,
> YOU WILL NEVER FIND IT
> IN YOUR PAST.

from the Pharisees and embraced his relationship with Zacchaeus.[8] He knew that Zacchaeus was the one who was going to *receive* his influence. Therefore it was fruitless to remain connected to those who would squander, disregard, or simply not recognize the favor and deliverance that stood before them. Jesus said it like this, *"He who receives you receives Me, and he who receives Me, receives Him who sent Me."*[9]

Receiving someone does not simply mean you accept them. Receiving someone has to do with embracing an individual's heart. I am *received* when an individual looks in my direction and extends favor to me.

---

8. See Luke 19:1-10
9. Matthew 10:40

How many times have we failed to receive from God because we did not recognize favor when it was extended to us? There may be many people who can benefit you, but there are only a few who have been strategically placed into your life to birth your future. The Apostle Paul told his Corinthian followers, *"You might have 10,000 instructors in Christ, but you have only one father. I am the one who has begotten you in the Gospel."*[10] You could have thousands of instructors, but those instructors may never be able to bring you to where you need to go.

People face enormous problems because they try to disconnect from relationships that they should keep, and keep relationships that should be terminated. Wisdom tells us that we need to have relationships in our lives that are actually *taking us somewhere*, not *keeping us from going somewhere*.

I must stop looking at my relationships emotionally, and evaluate my relationships according to what they do *to* me, what they do *with* me, and what they do *for* me. I must be willing to ask myself, "Is this a person that I can sow into, and know that tomorrow they are going to be a great, great tree in my life?"

Begin to filter out of your life those who don't add to you. You may need to make a clean sweep and start all over, with *nobody* in your life. That's fine! Once you have demolished the faulty foundations and eliminated the relationships that are sabotaging your future, you will then need to find the *right* people into whom you can begin to sow.

Remember, we must discard the idea of independence, and move toward *inter*dependence. We must realize that without one another we can never be promoted. Each one of us is part of the whole; there is nothing in your body that can survive alone. Your heart cannot live independently; neither can your brain. Each part of the body needs every other part in order to make it work. Who are the people that should be on your life team? Build a team, and then work within that team and through that team to bring promotion to your life and to theirs.

Every person needs *someone* in order to become what God wants him to become. Once again, your future is *completely linked* to the people and relationships that God has brought into your life.

10. 1 Corinthians 4:15, author's paraphrase

THE EXPONENTIAL POWER OF AGREEMENT

At first, you may find it uncomfortable to pursue others and sow into their lives. It's against man's nature to position himself with another human, because man wants to be his own god. But, Solomon spoke against independence when he said, *"A man who isolates himself seeks his own desire; He rages against all wise judgment."*[11] Jesus once said, *"For where two or three are gathered together in My name, I am there in the midst of them."*[12] He didn't say 'when you isolate yourself, I am there.'

The best thing I can do, if I want the exponential power of agreement working in my life, is to surround myself with people who unlock my faith and stand united with me in plan and purpose.

What I find very difficult to understand is that people do not see the importance of relationship. There can be absolutely no change in the world unless we *stick together!* Agreement and unity will cause the creativity and progress of any project to increase and accelerate at an unimaginable rate.

Never forget, friend, that *increase is normal and natural* in the economy of God. "Be fruitful and multiply" was the first instruction God gave to every living thing.[13] If you, *through your obedience,* are coming into agreement with Divine principles and precepts, then you can expect exponential blessing, increase, and promotion to come to you, through key relationships—it is the will of God for your life. That is the functioning of the Law of Synergy.

EVERYBODY NEEDS FOUR CRAZY FRIENDS

We often do not realize how vital these key relationships are, until a situation arises that would be irreparable and unable to be remedied, without the input and

11. Proverbs 18:1
12. Matthew 18:20
13. See Genesis 1:11, 12, 22

THE LAW OF SYNERGY | 217

efforts of those who love us. Mark once witnessed an incident that illustrates the life-altering importance of relationship:

> Several days later Jesus returned to Capernaum, and the news of his arrival spread quickly through the town. Soon the house where he was staying was so packed with visitors that there wasn't room for one more person, not even outside the door. And he preached the word to them. Four men arrived carrying a paralyzed man on a mat. They couldn't get to Jesus through the crowd, so they dug through the clay roof above his head. Then they lowered the sick man on his mat, right down in front of Jesus.[14]

The story goes on to say that when Jesus saw the faith of this man and his friends, He not only declared the man's sins forgiven, but physically healed him as well. The man jumped up, picked up his mat, and *walked* out of the house. This man's life was forever altered because of his relationship with four crazy friends who would not take "No" for an answer!

A dictionary study reveals that the word *crazy* means *wild, passionate, fanatic, and extreme*. We all need wild, passionate, and extreme people to motivate us to greatness. I call them "The Four Crazy Friends."

Just who are these relationships that you and I must pursue?

1. Those Who Motivate Your Obedience

You need someone in your life who motivates you to obey. Obedience brings prosperity and years of pleasantness to your life. Disobedience and recalcitrance bring ignorance and death.[15]

2. Those Who Are Guided By Their Character

Look for those who are self-correctors—those who live their lives according to the high standards of Divine principle. You will be greatly benefited by building relationship with those who refuse to tolerate double standards.

3. Those Who Defend You In Your Absence

A perfect example of this kind of friend would be Jonathan defending his friend, David, to his father, King Saul.[16] Do you have loyal friends who will not allow falsehoods against you to be perpetuated in their presence?

---

14. Mark 2:1-4, *NLT*
15. See Job 36:11-12, *NLT*
16. See 1 Samuel 20:30-34

4. Those Who Fear Heaven More Than They Love You

Whoever walks with the wise will become wise; whoever walks with fools will suffer harm.[17] You need someone who will not tiptoe around you, but will, when necessary, face off with you about your ethics and moral excellence. Don't seek people who want to please *you*; seek those who want to please God.

5. Those Who Motivate You To Sow

Sowing is the only way to get God's *movement and momentum* in your life. You need someone who will say, "Hey, let's help this child," or "Let's you and I build this widow a new home," or "Let's find shelter for this homeless mother." Have in your life individuals who will force you to keep your fist open to sow seed into other people's lives. *"Even when going through trouble and hard times themselves, their wonderful joy and deep poverty overflows in rich generosity."*[18]

6. Those Assigned To Your Future

Identify your "tomorrow people" and begin to *liberally* sow into their lives. *Actively* use your talents to promote them. Favor is summoned by your giving! If you don't have these people in your life, your life is all over.

7. Those Who Unlock Your Gratitude

Gratitude is *not* just appreciative words. True gratitude is spending the rest of your life *showing* someone your appreciation. Success and favor will chase you down when gratitude becomes the fragrance of your life.

If you will surround yourself with these kinds of relationships, you will find your life forever altered, as their influence and deposit cause you to stretch and pursue God's excellence and promotion in your life.

THE PROMOTIONAL POWER OF RELATIONSHIP

Many men and women look at their relationships in a *recreational* context, considering their purpose to be nothing deeper than simply providing "buddies"

---

17. Proverbs 13:20
18. 2 Corinthians 8:2, *NLT*, author's paraphrase

with which to have a good time. Superficial relationships such as these will not yield any benefit of eternal, lasting value.

God has very specific *reasons* for relationship. Because He has a special plan and purpose for your life, He also has special people who hold the keys to unlocking that plan and purpose. *These* are the people with whom God desires you to spend the rest of your life—the ones that He has chosen to promote and impact your future.

If intimacy does not give birth to change, then any future relationship is unnecessary. If you are not changing and growing as a result of your relationship, then what is the point of continuing it? Is there something beyond the fishing trips and the shopping sprees? Friend, don't let mediocrity penetrate your life through the influence of mediocre relationships! Such influence may appear benign, but like a cancer, it is indeed deadly.

> IF INTIMACY DOES NOT GIVE BIRTH TO CHANGE, THEN ANY FUTURE RELATIONSHIP IS UNNECESSARY.

If you are going to be thrust into a dynamic future, then you must surround yourself with dynamic, excellent individuals who might sometimes even make you feel *uncomfortable*. These individuals will compel you, by their very presence, to find the excellence within yourself.

SERVANTHOOD

Let's go back, once again, to the story of Elisha and Elijah. Each and every one of the sons of the prophets had the opportunity to be in the place of Elisha. Likewise, many of us are given opportunities that we often don't recognize, until they are gone. It may appear that you're getting nothing out of a particular association. It feels like you are the only one who is pouring into the relationship;

you're pouring and pouring and pouring and *pouring,* and nothing's happening—then, all of a sudden, everything climaxes and comes together so quickly, you wonder how it ever happened.

Just as Elisha was accosted by "nay-sayers" as he poured out his life in serving Elijah, you, too, may be approached by the 'sons of the prophets,' who will come to you and sneer, "You know, you're about to lose everything today. You know all that serving that you did? It hasn't done a thing for you, has it? All that laying down of your life...it was all a waste."

Never forget this, friend—servanthood is a high calling. It is *never* a waste. The only place that we will ever find our true identity is in serving. We'll never find it any other way. God did not call us *to be served.* He called us *to serve.*

The only way that I can discover who I am is to pick up the towel.[19] The moment that I realize I have a destiny, I need to go to the towel rack, because that's where my true identity is going to come from.

You can pursue success the world's way, or God's way. All you need to do is choose. The reason that many of us don't believe that God's way will work is that the people we've been watching have actually given up in the middle of the game, like the sons of the prophets did.

The Bible tells of a day when a large amount of people decided to give up on following Jesus.[20] Can you imagine having walked with Jesus for over three years, having gone through all of the pressures of being a disciple, having come to the end of Jesus' life, at the last supper, and *then* just turning away and saying, "You know what, that's it, I can't do it any more. I just can't do it."

Can you imagine the stories that all those people told, to justify their decision—the horror stories of not being able to receive, and how much of a lie it was to follow Jesus? I'm sure they spread their tales of how disappointing it was to have given up everything to follow the master, only to find out that he really wasn't who he said he was, and his words weren't really true. And now, their lives were wrecked, disappointed, disillusioned, without any future and without any hope. And Jesus turned to the twelve disciples and said, "Well, are you going to go, too?"

19. See John 13:4-5
20. See John 6:66

And this is the point where some of you might be sitting today. "Are you going to give up, too?"

The sons of the prophets couldn't commit. They wouldn't take the risk to make a promise or a covenant. So, they remained *sons* of prophets *only*. They continued to sound and look really good—but they were *never fulfilled*. They never stepped into their destiny.

And so, the sons of the prophets, the ones who couldn't leave it all behind, said, "Don't you know that your master will be taken away today?"

And Elisha responded by saying, "Yea, I know it, shut your mouth. I don't want to hear it from you. I don't want to hear about how I can stay with you and *you'll* make me somebody. This relationship that I have with Elijah is not going to die!"

When they finally came to the end, Elijah asked Elisha, "What can I do for you? What is it that you want from me? What would you like? What is it that you're after?"

And Elisha said, "Well, you know I've looked at you for all these years…I've followed you—I've studied you—I've watched you—I've served you. **I just want to be you, times two.**" Even when it came time for *his* promotion, Elisha was still saying to his mentor, "I want to multiply *you*. I want to multiply *your life*. I want to make *you* live again."

How many of us have ever stood at a casket and said, "If I could only give you my time, so you could live again." *You can*—but not in the way that you may think. If you have been a true son, the father who has poured himself into you *lives again through you*. The world still enjoys his presence and is still able to eat of the fruit of his life, because you'll offer it to the world through *your* life.

Elisha said, "Master, all that I want is to be you *twice over*."

And Elijah answered, "You know, you're asking something really hard, because this is not a request that has a human answer. You've gotten into the Divine, (which, incidentally, is *exactly* where you need to go.)" And he continued, "I can't do that for you, but I'll tell you this. When I leave, if you see my mantle coming down, then you'll have the request that you desire."

And as the whirlwind took Elijah away, the mantle began to come down from heaven, and Elisha cried out, "My father! My father!"

People have the idea that what Elisha was expressing as he cried out was, "My father, my father, look, praise the Lord, I got your mantle! I'm going to perform twice the miracles that you ever performed!"

But, notice what Elisha did next. When the mantle hit the ground, Elisha ripped his clothes in two, stripped naked, picked up Elijah's clothes, put them on, and said these words, "Now, where is *the Lord God of Elijah?*" Then he took the mantle, smote the river with it, and walked across on dry ground.

Elisha had now become *a carrier of Elijah's influence upon the earth.* Because of the intimacy of their relationship and the obedience of the son, the favor, excellence, and fingerprint of the father would now continue, expand, and be passed on to a thousand generations through his faithful servant.

You see, the very thing that God wants to bring you, through the synergy of relationship, is *multiplication.* He wants to bring you *generational blessing, favor, and promotion.* He wants to bring you to a place where you can multiply the life of the person at whose feet you sit. Why? Because God is going to have someone else to sit at *your* feet! But He will not trust that person to just anyone. *He will trust him only to one who has already bowed his knee to the heart of another.*

PREPARATION

Submitting to the heart of another is an essential test in preparing your heart for your moment of promotion. Do not focus on creating a promotion for yourself. *God knows how to create a need that you can fill.* Your assignment is to *prepare your heart and pursue excellence*—and excellence is the continual pursuit of **distinction.**

Remember, favor is granted to you the moment that someone discovers your difference and needs what you have. But your 'difference' doesn't simply materialize to fit a situation; your difference exists *first*, and *then* the situation comes. *Only when you have already prepared*, are you able to step into that situation and fill that need. *We cannot enter our future when we are chained to our past by our lack of preparation.* You must prepare *now*, so that you are ready when your moment of promotion arrives. Remember, you never have a second chance at a first impression!

> EXCELLENCE IS THE CONTINUAL PURSUIT OF *DISTINCTION*.

God is looking for you to *prepare*. You see, if you merely focus upon what you have today, you will never realize what God has for your future. You will not get the promotion that God has planned for you, because, by your lethargic preparation, you are indicating that you really don't believe that He's taking you any further than you are right now. That's why people go 5, 10, 15 years and never change. They aren't convinced that God wants them to be greater. But, the truth is that everything that God has created is designed to grow. Anything God touches is destined to multiply.

As you grow, there are increasingly greater levels of responsibility and challenge. When you first start out, the difficulty levels are relatively easy, and God gives you quick, decisive victories. But the day arrives when you meet your match—the day when you discover your enemy; and now God wants you to be victorious over your enemy.

> WE CANNOT ENTER OUR FUTURE WHEN WE ARE CHAINED TO OUR PAST BY OUR LACK OF PREPARATION.

Perhaps you have heard the expression, "Greater levels, greater devils." It's a funny little saying, but it's the truth. The more that you grow and move towards fulfilling the purpose for your life, the more the enemy of your promotion will come to you and say, "You're not going to do that." And you have to realize that, if he says it, you have to prove him wrong.

This is the reason that relationships are *so important* to you—*the people who are in front of you know how to beat what you're facing.* But, if you are by yourself, you'll never know how to beat the enemies that taunt you. Don't waste the years of your life, friend. Life is designed in such a way that if you want to learn things *on your own*, you will always have just a little bit less time than your ability to produce, and you will live unfulfilled. But if you'll take someone else's word for it, and become compliant, God will change your life.

As well as levels of responsibility and challenge, there are also different levels of performance. Lower-level performance will actually teach you principles and show you how you can do something for yourself. But higher-level performance kicks in the moment that you have reached the pinnacle of your own potential. At that point, God can use the potential of another to promote you and to take you to a level that you could have never achieved on your own. This is multiplication through association, and the essence of how the Law of Synergy works.

> GOD WILL USE THE POTENTIAL OF ANOTHER TO TAKE YOU TO A LEVEL THAT YOU COULD NEVER ACHIEVE ON YOUR OWN.

I recognize that I passed my potential a long time ago. Now, I'm receiving and operating in the potential of my superiors. This is called *favor*; someone wants to participate in the productivity of my future. I had to come to the point where I realized that it was not wrong for someone to promote me far beyond my potential. I didn't need to fear or question the promotion since I had prepared my heart.

SOWING

Sowing is the foundation of preparation. As we've already discussed, what you do *first* will determine how anything in life responds to you. The one who invests first, in relationship, is the one who has the relationship responding to him. Are there tears in this kind of sowing? You'd better believe it. Is there disappointment?

Yes, because of the inability and reluctance of many people to respond. (Whether they realize it or not, because of the pain of their past, they are stagnant.) However, their unwillingness to respond only shows you *to whom you are not assigned.* And rest assured, at times you may not reap *where* you sow, but once again, *you will always reap what you sow.*

When you first begin to pursue someone who might be a key to your future, you need to go at it three or four times, because they need to know that you're serious. But after several attempts, if that individual does not respond to the sowing you've done in their lives, do not be discouraged. You have now simply discovered someone to whom you are *not* assigned.

This may surprise you, but the people that I'm in relationship with are not necessarily the people that are my cup of tea when it comes to personality. But they are the people *that responded* to my pursuit, and I have found my life being greatly multiplied because I pursued those relationships and they responded. They weren't necessarily the people that I had envisioned would respond. Truthfully, I wanted others who I thought were right for me, to respond as well, but they didn't. Does that mean there is something wrong with me? Absolutely not! God knows from which ground my seed will yield its harvest!

But, nothing happens until you *enter* the pursuit. You have to engage. You cannot hope to get a response unless and until you engage. Even though it is risky, and you may feel exposed and vulnerable, you must wrap your faith around your seed and begin to sow! That's why *"they that sow in tears shall reap in joy. They go forth weeping, bearing precious seed..."*[21] As you know, *it's precious.*

Thoughts may run through your mind, "You never should have done that, nothing is ever going to come of that seed," or "You never should have risked being disappointed in this relationship." And if you listen to these lies, you'll end up ten years down the line, exactly the same as you are today—because you would not take the risk.

Remember, friend, anything that has the potential for value or victory in your life also carries the potential for loss. Intrinsic to the pursuit of any excellent rela-

---

21. Psalm 126:5-6, author's paraphrase

tionship is the risk that the pursuit will bear no fruit. And that is a choice that you must make. Are you willing to sow in tears? Are you willing to go forth weeping, bearing precious seed? You will have to use *yourself* as a seed, because that's the only way you will ever be able to realize the maximum amount of fruitfulness from your life.

THE ABILITY TO CONCEIVE IN RELATIONSHIP

There are provisions and promotions available within the womb of key relationships that are unattainable through isolationism or superficial associations. *Today's provision* may come through *diligence*, but *tomorrow's promotion* can only come through *relationship*. The dili-

> TODAY'S PROVISION
> MAY COME THROUGH
> DILIGENCE, BUT
> TOMORROW'S PROMOTION
> CAN ONLY COME THROUGH
> RELATIONSHIP.

gent work of one man can never match the production that flows from the synergy of relationship. In addition, God may miraculously provide for you momentarily, but He does not want you needing to live from miracle to miracle. He will show you key relationships that you must *pursue* and *be committed to,* in order to unlock the seed for your future.

Many people enter a relationship intending to stay only for as long as it benefits them. As long as they operate with this attitude, they are actually planting the seeds of miscarriages and abortions in their own lives. They may be excited about their dream or vision, but somehow they are never able to birth that dream into a reality. This barrenness exists because they have *never conceived* out of relationship.

God designed *conception and reproduction* to take place in *relationship*. Often, when it comes to the arena of relationships, we want to link up to a person that we think is 'cool.' But, I've realized that the people who I thought were the 'coolest' were not the people that actually had the potential to birth my future. They could not help me enter the next realm of my life. They were unwilling to receive my seed in order for it to conceive and bring forth fruit.

> MY FUTURE LIES IN MY PROMPTNESS TO COMPLETE A REQUEST FROM THE ONE WHO HAS SHOWN ME FAVOR.

But, when I discover a key individual who will receive my seed and open a door of favor to me, I run through that door at 1000 miles an hour, *always at attention*, because that's where my future lies.

So, here is the sequence for birthing your desired future —

* Pursue a 'future bearer' and sow your seed with tears.
* Someone will receive your seed and open a door of favor to you. *This is the moment of conception.*
* Obediently and excellently complete the task/tasks given to you by the one who has shown you favor.
* Your promotion and future are birthed.

Disobedience is the abortifacient or abortion-inducing agent that threatens the birth of God's plan in your life. At any point, this whole birthing process could be terminated if you turn your back on obedience, submission, honor, or respect.

ACTIVATING "THE RIPPLE EFFECT"

When I embrace the wisdom and advice of those who have gone on before me, I guarantee the future of my relationship. I can literally document my obedience by actually going down a list, saying, "You said to do this; I did this. You said to do that; I did that." Suddenly, my life begins to *exponentially multiply.*

When you move in these realms of relational excellence, you are not only *pursuing* influencers, but you have *become an influencer.* You have gotten the Law of Synergy to work for you, and you are multiplying your life to affect a thousand generations. You have thrown the seed/pebble of your life into the water of time, and have started a ripple effect that will expand and continue throughout eternity.

As you become a leader and an influencer, God will desire to use you to extend favor and promotion to others. You will become a 'future bearer' in the life of other individuals who will pursue you and begin to sow their precious seed into *you*.

When your influence begins to change the life of an individual, you are not changing the destiny of just one person. That one person will catch your fire, and start his own concentric ripple. And every person that he touches will do the same. Your life will then impact the temporal and eternal futures of thousands.

There is no greater reward in this life than knowing that the seed of your life is being multiplied and extended for generations, through those who have sat at your feet and embraced the essence of your heart. Never forget how precious and valuable each of those people are, in the eyes of God.

Here is how you activate "The Ripple Effect" in the life of the people you touch:

1. Demonstrate that they are important and valuable.

2. Prove to them that they are cared for and protected.

3. Show them that they are heard and understood.

4. Affirm and appreciate them.

5. When a person feels all of the above, he will be motivated to pursue his or her highest potential, making an impact in your life and in the life of others.

6. By activating this *ripple effect*, you will not just change *one life*. As you bring exponential, multiplying power to each life you touch, *you will eternally change the destiny of multitudes.*

THE SIMPLICITY OF SYNERGY

God never wanted us to walk alone. He actually wants us to walk with someone else, for then, if one of us has a problem, the other one can pick him up.[22] When I discovered this, I began to search for *what I could do for others*, and how I could help them fulfill their assignments.

What is your assignment? You need other people to help you fulfill it. But, you can never reap a crop of having others help you fulfill *your* call, until you have first helped them fulfill *their* call. Get active in helping someone else get over the finish line, and then you can get in line yourself. But here is an interesting paradox: The one who just crossed over the finish line in life, is *now able and willing to push you*. He *knows* how to help you win! You don't have to do it all on your own.

It's amazingly simple! It's so simple, that I had to back up to understand it! These principles speak about *serving other people*—most people spend 23 hours and 55 minutes every day serving themselves. But, be assured, you will not find any life, joy, or favor at all, until you stop focusing on your own interests and start doing what others need you to do. Then, and only then, will you be able to activate the supernatural law of relational synergy.

---

22. See Ecclesiastes 4:9-12

THE LAW OF SYNERGY

One can chase a thousand,
but two will put ten thousand to flight!

+ In order to have a relationship with one, you just may have to disconnect from another.

+ When you are looking for your future, you will never find it in your past.

+ If intimacy does not give birth to change, then any future relationship is unnecessary.

+ Excellence is the continual pursuit of *distinction.*

+ We cannot enter our future when we are chained to our past by our lack of preparation.

+ God will use the potential of another to take you to a level that you could never achieve on your own.

+ Today's provision may come through diligence, but tomorrow's promotion can only come through relationship.

+ My future lies in my promptness to complete a request from the one who has shown me favor.

THE LAW OF
ASCENT

WALK WITH THE GREAT,
AND YOU WILL BECOME GREAT.

10

WALK WITH THE GREAT,

AND YOU WILL BECOME GREAT.

As the favor and promotion of your relationships begin to synergistically compound and multiply, you will find yourself on a steady climb of ascent. In surrounding yourself with those who walk in excellence and have empires within them, the borders of your own dreams will be enlarged. As you sow your life to advance their ascendancy, you, too, will advance, for you have inexorably tied yourself to the same standard of excellence.

COMPLY WITH GREATNESS

Relationships with great individuals are your doorways to a great future. You must pursue these relationships, not so that their greatness will "rub off" on you, but so that you can have good, fertile ground in which to sow your seed. But there

> IN ORDER TO GET
> CLOSE TO GREATNESS,
> I MUST COMPLY
> WITH GREATNESS.

are prerequisites to entering into relationship with those who are excellent. *In order to get close to greatness, I must comply with greatness.*

The people who you are with reflect your level of achievement in life. If you keep living like the people that you were with yesterday, you'll never be able to embrace the people of greatness for your tomorrow. Your direction in life is proven by the people who are willing to spend time with you. You've got to seed yourself into the lives of great people, and then you must stay in faith.

Every level of intimacy has qualifications. When Jesus began His ministry, there were multitudes following him. We then hear that there were 500 disciples. Within those, there were 70, and from those there were 12 Apostles. From the 12, He had an inner circle of 3. And then there was John, concerning whom it was written, *"the disciple whom Jesus loved."*[1] Jesus had clear levels of intimacy. But rest assured that there were qualifications for every level. In order to get great individuals to go into a deeper relationship with *you,* you have to demonstrate to them that you desire to passionately pursue a deeper relationship with *them.*

The beginning of a relationship is dependent upon the *giver of favor* in that relationship. The maintenance and continuance, however, is completely dependent upon the *receiver of favor* in that relationship. As a mentor, I may desire to open a door for someone, but *keeping it open* is completely dependent upon the other person's posture and productivity. I can open a door for an individual, but I cannot indefinitely keep it open without a response or performance from him. Whether or not he walks through that door or maintains the relationship is completely dependent upon his performance and his understanding of the favor that I've shown him.

In parental relationships (again, both natural and spiritual) a father's greatest desire is to have a compliant son that he can pour himself into. But, once he has opened the door and extended the favor, the future of that relationship is dependent

---

1. See John 13: 23, 20: 2, and 21: 20

upon the hunger of the son. The authenticity of the son's desire is expressed through his pursuit; conversely, the proof of a son's indifference is expressed through his lack of pursuit.

A son who is passionate about conforming to greatness is a son whose heart is soft, pliable, and easily molded. He is *ready* to receive the distinctive fingerprint of his father, and to forever be identified with that signature. He wants to become the vessel that will carry his father's greatness into coming generations. And he welcomes the discipline and correction needed to make him a vessel worthy of that honor.

I quickly realized that my willingness to receive and embrace correction from my fathers opened doors of intimacy with them. Once I got on the same side of the table as those who were correcting me, they no longer could point their finger at me. Instead, they began to say, "Now come close, there is something I've got to show you." Now I was ready to be *instructed*. They took me into their lives and started showing me the secret things of their hearts, the keys that no one else ever got.

We must remember that intimacy and promotion was God's idea, not man's. The plan of God is that the influence of a great man would continue beyond himself, through his sons and daughters, and into future generations. The impartation of such greatness and influence is only possible through *relationship*. It is the *intimacy of relationship* that facilitates not just the transfer of *information*, but also the world-changing power of *transformation*.

THOSE WHO SEE WHAT I CANNOT SEE

There is something about a father that you must know. A father does not care about the acceptance of the son. A father is more interested in your *freedom* than he is in your *friendship*. Now, if you start walking in freedom, and friendship develops beyond that, that's wonderful; but friendship can never take the place of freedom. One must learn how to posture as a son or a daughter, for you can never be a parent if you have not yet become a son. You cannot teach others if you have not, yourself, embraced the wisdom of your teachers.

Contrary to popular belief, experience is not the best teacher. A wise son will learn from his father's mistakes, but a fool won't even learn from his own! *Consequences are the detentions you receive when you refuse to sit at the feet of an instructor.*

> CONSEQUENCES ARE THE DETENTIONS YOU RECEIVE WHEN YOU REFUSE TO SIT AT THE FEET OF AN INSTRUCTOR.

Never insist on having to learn the lessons of life "on your own." The hard-earned wisdom of an entire generation is completely discarded when sons refuse to listen; and then the whole ugly cycle of unwanted experiences once again repeats itself. Be a wise son who chooses his father's wisdom rather than the detentions and penalties of experience. Those who have gone before you and poured their life's blood into giving you a head start have already built the foundations for you —all you have to do is *continue building.*

When you are young and eager to build a future for yourself, you become extremely focused and understandably fixated on fulfilling your purpose in life. Focus is a good attribute, but realize that it also blinds you. When you focus on north, someone else must see south. Seek the perspective of those with an eagle-eye view.

> WISDOM IS THE REWARD PROVIDED FOR THOSE WHO WALK IN HUMILITY.

Do not hesitate to ask others to speak their discoveries aloud for your consideration. The circle of counsel whose advice you pursue will decide the amount of success you experience.

We must remember that those who walk ahead of us on this journey through life can see things that we cannot see. If we are wise, and want to be protected from traps that have been set for us, we will trust their insight and follow their directions implicitly.

There once was a man called Naaman who had been healed of leprosy through Elisha's intervention. Elisha gave clear direction to his servant Gehazi, instructing him *not* to receive the gifts of gratitude from Naaman. But in his greed and impatience for promotion, Gehazi disobeyed Elisha and took the silver and clothing, hiding them in his house. When he went and stood before his master, Elisha said to him, "Where have you been Gehazi?"

Gehazi lied, saying, " I haven't been anywhere."

But Elisha knew otherwise, "Is now the time, Gehazi? I told you it wasn't. Is now the time?"

"I thought it was," stammered Gehazi, guiltily.

"Didn't you wonder why I didn't receive those clothes from the hand of Naaman, Gehazi? *I saw something you did not see—I knew something you did not know.* You touched those clothes, and now the leprosy that was bound to the life of Naaman is bound to you and your family forever! And this is all because you wanted the right thing, but you just wanted it at the wrong time." And when Gehazi left the room, his skin became leprous.[2]

I have learned to trust the discernment and judgment of my authorities, especially in matters of timing and promotion. They have helped me to see that when I thought I was ready, I really wasn't. And it was when I said that I wasn't ready, that they knew I truly *was*. When I barely had any more passion for it, God brought it to me, but He brought it to me *in the midst of my commitment to my fathers.*

The greatest comfort that you'll ever know is to have a father in your life. The greatest understanding that you'll ever experience will come as a result of embracing and honoring your mentor. You must, however, embrace your father with an honorable motive.

Immediate, short-term blessing is what is foremost in the mind of a taker or a prodigal. The bastard is only interested in the *blessing* of a father; the son is

2. See 2 Kings 5, author's paraphrase

> THE BASTARD IS ONLY INTERESTED IN THE BLESSING OF A FATHER; THE SON IS INTERESTED IN THE INHERITANCE OF HIS FATHER.

interested in the *inheritance* of his father. Gehazi was interested in the material gifts that Naaman could give. The true sons are interested in the *inheritance* of their fathers, namely *greatness, vision, anointing, victory, wisdom, and excellence.*

Esau was another man who was willing to trade his future away for short-term gratification. His response was, "What good is this birthright to me, anyway."[3] And therein lies the attitude in many people's hearts. It's the attitude that says, "Look, all I'm interested in is what I can eat today, and what I can get out of this right now."

So, Esau's brother Jacob gave him a bowl of stew in exchange for the birthright. From that moment forward, God's hand was upon Jacob rather than Esau. Jacob saw value in the inheritance, while Esau only wanted short-term gratification and blessing.

If you desire to receive an inheritance from the life of another, you must passionately pursue that inheritance. You pursue the inheritance by esteeming the *giver* higher than you esteem the *gift.* You must pursue the relationship *not* for what you can get out of it, but for what you can deposit inside of it.

Many people enter this type of relationship with a "user" mentality. For example, when they buy a set of teaching tapes, they only want the information, not the teacher.

On the other hand, there are those who will pursue a *relationship* with the teacher. The teacher's information may not necessarily be quite as good as someone else's, but there is something different about *him* that draws them to a relationship. In pursuing that relationship, they are more interested in what they can *inherit* from the teacher, than in merely experiencing short-term gain.

When I embrace those who see what I cannot see, I am ensuring my future. The foresight and wisdom of those who have pioneered the trail ahead of me will

3. Genesis 25:32, author's paraphrase

protect me from ignorant mistakes and preserve me from the ambush of my ene-mies. I am, therefore, preserved and able to carry the inheritance of my father's influence into the next generation.

CHARACTER: THE DETERMINER OF ASCENT

As a son and a protégé, I have a responsibility in the relationships I pursue. That responsibility must lead me to bow my knee to authority, because that is the only way that I can be promoted. I must readily *position myself as a learner,* and not be so quick to think that I have all the answers. *I must always remember that my posture will determine my ascent.*

Let us create a possibly fictional sce-nario: let us momentarily pretend that you are a wiz-kid at the company that you work for. However, in spite of your expertise, you are consistently giving them disappointment, through a poor attitude. The company then has a choice whether or not to retain you, or to put their finances, training, and future into the hands of someone more teachable. Which one will they choose? My guess is they would let you go and hire someone with a good atti-tude. *A good attitude far outweighs ability every time.* You can train someone who has a good attitude, but a bad attitude is simply bad character *expressed*—and char-acter is much more difficult to adjust.

> YOUR POSTURE WILL DETERMINE YOUR ASCENT

As reported in the book *The Millionaire Mind,*[4] there was a survey conducted in which both millionaires and middle class men were asked, "What kind of girl are you looking for, when you marry?" The number one attribute that the middle class men were looking for, in a potential spouse, was good looks. In the million-aire's mind, the number one attribute of a good wife was good character. Good looks was number nine on the millionaires' list. This survey confirms that most

---

4. Thomas J. Stanley, *The Millionaire Mind* (Kansas City, MO: Andrews McMeel Publishing, 2000), p. 250-251.

people do not realize how important good character really is! Long after things begin to sag in all directions, and shape themselves in different ways, *character still remains.* Character doesn't go away.

I observe that many of the people that I associate with really don't understand the value of character. Yet, nothing good can ever be built in a person's life without good character. As we have already discussed, work at fixing character in your life before you attempt to work on anything else, or you will end up being a failure. You will begin to build, and it will be broken down. You'll build again, and someone else will plow it down. You'll build yet again, and someone will steal it from you, because of your gullibility to other's lack of character.

If you want to know something about a person, don't ask questions; just study his friends. When you ask questions, people can lie. But watching with whom a person associates will reveal the truth. Just study them. Look at their character, observe their whereabouts, watch the kind of things they do, and find out if there is any compromise within their lives. Take a good look at the people who surround an individual, and you will discover a lot about him. A person's direction in life is proven by whomever his friends are.

> YOU WILL BE BOTH BLESSED BY THE VIRTUES AND CURSED BY THE VICES OF THOSE CLOSEST TO YOU.

Many people object to this type of character 'yardstick.' They tell me, "But Dr. Thompson, these people don't have any affect on me. We just hang out, they are not really my friends." No, *you are them.* You will be both blessed by the virtues and cursed by the vices of those closest to you.

Other people actually enjoy associating with a bunch of failures, because it makes them look good, by comparison. They know how to spout words of excellence with their mouth, but they don't have to perform. Performance is not required when you surround yourself with mediocrity.

There are also those who attempt to associate with the great because of the awesome power of transferred credibility. This is truly diabolical.

However, in my circle of relationships, the substance of who you are is not in what you say; *everything is performance.* A man is not defined by his beliefs, but by the quality of his actions. "I just want to see what you're going to do. I don't want to hear what you believe, because you don't believe what you say—you only believe *what you do. I'm going to watch what you do.* If I see inconsistencies, I will love you enough to tell you."

> A MAN IS NOT DEFINED BY HIS BELIEFS, BUT BY THE QUALITY OF HIS ACTIONS.

Even a person of strong, virtuous character needs someone else to "watch his back" and speak into his life concerning any weak areas. A person who has nine hundred ninety-nine strong points in life can get quite upset when you want to talk to him about his one weak point. But, if you truly care for that person, you will address it, for even a chain that has nine hundred ninety-nine strong links *is no stronger than it's weakest link.* That chain is disqualified, not because of its nine hundred ninety-nine strong links, but because of its single weak one! *For our own protection,* we all need someone to whom we can be accountable, in the arena of character.

> YOUR CHARACTER IS THE FOUNDATION UPON WHICH YOUR LIFE'S WORK IS BUILT.

What is character? *Your character is the foundation upon which your life's work is built.* Character is virtue in the life of an individual. Character is moral strength and moral constitution. Character is a reputation of integrity built by the hard choices of self-sacrifice and self-discipline. Character affects our decisions, our words, our attitudes, our goals, our relationships, and our actions. Character is the summation of the principles down on the inside of us, by which we live our lives.

In marriage, character is gentleness.

In the home, it is respect.

In business, it is integrity.

In society, it is courtesy.

In the workplace, it is excellence.

In sports, it is fairness.

In relationship, it is kindness.

To the victor, it is congratulations.

To the victim, it is protection.

To falsehood, it is resistance.

To the less fortunate, it is a hand up.

To the strong, it is trust.

To the repentant, it is restoration.

To yourself, it is absolute truth.

And to God, it is reverence, love and commitment.

PRESSING TOWARD THE MARK

A person of character is continually changing. He realizes that the more influential he becomes, the deeper his influence bleeds into generations of people to come. *He knows that what he says and does matters,* so he is motivated to *push* and make his best even better.

When things are going well in your life, you need to push hard and make huge strides. Don't get caught in the trap of thinking, "Things are fine right now, so I'll just coast." No! It's when things are going well that you are able to eat up a lot of ground and press forward. Let time become your friend, instead of your enemy.

You can do one of two things with your time. You can either *pass/kill time,* or you can *invest it.* Always choose to invest. Choose to whom you are going to give your time. *Choose*—because everything you do is a *choice*. Do not allow yourself to be drawn along in the current of what's going on with everyone else around you.

Keeping in mind that you are pursuing excellence, *you choose* what you want to do with your time. You make the choice so that you can stand before God and say, "Yes sir, I am responsible for my choices, for I made them."

> **TODAY'S EXCELLENCE IS TOMORROW'S MEDIOCRITY.**

Today's excellence is tomorrow's mediocrity. Winning and becoming excellent in life is really very simple. All you need to do is choose to give up all your mediocrities. It's not hard, but it's got to be *real*. You see, God is looking for where you *live;* He's not looking for where you *talk*. God is looking for the *realities* in your heart, not the things that you *tell* others that you believe. He's not listening to what you *proclaim;* He's watching what you *produce.*

Personally, I need to squeeze all of the life and all of the productivity out of these next forty years. Now, I can't do that if I play. So when I give, I give hard. When I love, I love hard. When I follow, I follow hard. There are people who say, "Robb, you are so intense."

I respond, "You haven't seen anything yet!" I am very serious about what God wants to do through my life. I'm very serious about tomorrow, and I recognize that if I mess up today, I may as well erase tomorrow.

We must show diligence in handling our present assignments, because until we commendably take care of the things that we have right in front of us, God can never really promote us. Until we are overqualified for our present responsibilities, God will never assign new ones to us.

> **IT IS IMPOSSIBLE TO CORRECT WHAT YOU ARE UNWILLING TO FACE.**

Never stop changing and never stop pressing. The moment that you stop moving and start camping, you are in trouble. Being resistant to change indicates inflexibility and an unwillingness to submit, subject, or adapt. Anything that is inflexible is brittle and easily broken. Remember: *It is impossible to correct what you are unwilling to face.*

What happens is that people fight, struggle, push, kick, scratch, and punch

> IT IS IMPOSSIBLE
> FOR YOUR LIFE TO PRODUCE
> ANYTHING BEYOND THE
> STRENGTH OF YOUR
> MORAL FIBER.

their way to a particular level, and then say, "That's enough—I don't want to move anymore. I don't want to change anymore. I don't want to dismantle my life anymore." You are now in a rut, which is a grave with the ends kicked out!

The Apostle Paul exhorted his friends,

Therefore, since we have so great a cloud of witnesses surrounding us, let us also lay aside every encumbrance, and the sin which so easily entangles us, and let us run with endurance the race that is set before us...[5]

From the original Greek, this verse could be understood to say, "...lay down and push far away (beyond reach) everything that weighs you down, including the environment that so comfortably envelops you..."[6]

Comfort is an enemy to anyone who desires to fulfill his greatest potential. Comfort entices you to take your ease and to no longer press. Mediocrity pursues comfort, while excellence pursues change. If you desire to be a winner, you must continually assess your environment, making certain that old thinking, old friends, or old ways are not weighing you down and preventing you from rising to the soaring levels that God wants to take you.

You've got to keep pressing, and building, and risking, and growing. But you need to do it in front of the people who know you, who have invested in you, and

> MEDIOCRITY
> PURSUES COMFORT, WHILE
> EXCELLENCE PURSUES
> CHANGE.

who have loved you the most. Refuse to go into a corner and attempt to do it alone. In order to keep yourself protected, and to make a difference in other's lives, your life must be lived before people and not in isolation.

Success is not the fairy tale state of bliss that Hollywood would have us believe. Success is the willingness to bear pain. It is the self-discipline of consistently train-

5. Hebrews 12:1, *NAS*
6. Rick Renner, *Sparkling Gems from the Greek* (Tulsa, OK: Teach All Nations, 2003), p. 51-52, 113-114.

ing yourself. Training. Training. Training to the point where pain doesn't bother you anymore. It doesn't matter what you are going through or how hurtful people may become. You have trained yourself in mental alertness and moral strength of character. You are not going to be moved, no matter what anyone says and no matter what anyone does.

STRONG WHERE I AM WEAK

The easiest way for me to train and to grow as a person is to surround myself with people who are smarter than I am. These are people who:

* Are assigned to my future
* Motivate me to pursue
* Unlock my gratitude
* Are ethically driven
* Fear God more than they love me
* Motivate me to sow
* Make me grow

When you assume the posture of a student, especially with those who are strong in arenas where you are weak, you immediately begin to mature and bear fruit.

Submission to authority is the avenue through which my character is developed.
The fruit of my submission is character, the fruit of my character is dignity, and the fruit of my dignity is righteousness.

This process does not happen overnight. It takes time to walk in righteousness. But we must remember that excellence is not a destination; it's a journey.

> SUBMISSION
> TO AUTHORITY IS
> THE AVENUE THROUGH
> WHICH MY CHARACTER
> IS DEVELOPED.

It's a process! And this process of growth stops the moment that you reject beneficial relationships.

Often, we only want people in our lives when things are going bad; we are willing to allow others in when we're having a tough night. The deception is that we don't need others when everything seems to be sailing—when we are working at it, and making it, and things look like they are running on all eight cylinders.

Friend, learn how to allow people to be part of your life when things are going well; because as soon as success and promotion come, you will need to function at a greater level of difficulty, and it's at those moments that you *most* need the influence of a mentor in your life. It is at this time that you will need to reach out into the pool of already established relationships, for their much needed support and direction.

Do you remember when you were eight-years-old and played baseball in little league? You were the biggest kid in the league, since all the other players were between six and eight-years-old. You could hit and field the ball, and the other children couldn't. Maybe you'd hit the ball only 40 feet, but you'd get a home run every time! But then, all of a sudden you had a birthday. And when you turned nine-years-old, you now were in a league that was for nine to twelve-year-olds. So, instead of being the big fish in a little pond, you now were the little fish in a big pond! Overnight, your level of difficulty grew, and you had to work through a couple of years before you could be the "best man on the team" again. You had to go through a period of humility before you ever got to greatness once again. The process of advancement in life works the same way. Any time that we become successful at something, greater responsibility is given to us.

> WITH EVERY
> PROMOTION COMES GREATER
> RESPONSIBILITY.

To receive advancement without an increase would be a contradiction in terms. Rarely do promotions come with more money. They come with a *promise* of more money, and then you have to roll up your sleeves and chase it till you get it! But they *always* come with more responsibility, over which you must be faithful.

Whenever you show yourself to be faithful and successful, God takes you to another level. At that new level, you will face moments of *anything but* success, because you are learning how to conquer the giants that live at that new level. And though possibly still undiscovered to you, God has already placed people in front of you who have already faced and beaten devils whose names you haven't even learned yet. If you are wise, you will make a draw on their expertise.

Whenever I hit a bump, the *first* thing I do is ask for help. I inquire, "Can you please help me with this?" Rather than sitting there, struggling with it, and wringing my hands, saying, "Oh my God, what am I going to do," I call someone on the telephone and say, "Sir, do you have any notes on this subject?"

You'd be amazed at the people that call me for my notes on subjects! And quite often I am sure some of these individuals would have better notes than mine. But, truthfully, someone else has already been where I am going. In fact, there isn't anything that I've ever achieved, that someone hasn't *helped me* to achieve. I didn't really make any of this happen on my own. I have developed the skills of bowing my knee, asking for help, and positioning myself as a learner. I *listen carefully* to the instruction, and then follow it to a 't'; and I do all this without trying to distance myself from the one who instructed me.

The foundation stone for building *any* fruitful relationship is the ability to *effectively listen.* The first symptom of a closed mind and heart is someone who will not listen. This world is full of talkers and very few listeners. Therefore, everyone is starved for someone to listen to *them.* If you are a good listener, others will be *drawn* to you, and when you do speak, people will sit up and take notice to what you are saying.

Keep in mind that someone who postures as a good student is, for the most part, in listening mode. A student knows that his future success is completely dependent on his willingness to listen. He understands that someone out there knows something that he should know, and that one tiny piece of information can turn his failures into a success.

You cannot position as an "expert" and still continue to reap the benefits of a student. Such an attitude guarantees that learning, growth, and improvement come to a halt. Instead, position as a student in every conversation, and search out what *others* know that *you have yet to discover.* Put your whole attention on them and what they are saying. Purpose that your conversations with others will be the first place that you demonstrate respect and *humility.*

> GREATNESS BECOMES YOURS THE MOMENT YOU BECOME SMALL IN YOUR OWN EYES.

Greatness becomes yours the moment you become small in your own eyes. Remember, the *willingness to reach is the proof of humility.* Many people get a few accomplishments under their belt and then become too proud to posture as a learner. But your pride is the sacrifice that is laid upon the altar of humility. As you choose to walk in humility, wisdom will be your reward, and greatness will be your future.

NEVER GIVE UP

Solomon once said, *"Do you see a man who excels in his work? He will stand before kings; He will not stand before unknown men."*[7] A man who excels in his work is a man who never gives up. He may get knocked down thousands of times, but he never stays down—he always gets back up. You will never stand in front of kings if you are a quitter.

Pursuing and maintaining relationships with great, distinctive people is not an endeavor for dropouts. Demands and expectations are placed upon a pursuer that will quickly filter and eliminate all but the most resolute and devoted.

There comes a day, in every relationship, where a promise needs to be made. Every relationship comes to promises, and when it finally does, there are many that

---

7. Proverbs 22:29

cannot make the commitment—so they give up the pursuit, and they give up the relationship. They stay right where they are and never advance or grow beyond that point.

The day came when Elijah said to Elisha, "Stay here, because the Lord has sent me to Jericho." Jericho represented *the point of no return*. It's the place where you know that you can no longer go back. And now you are facing the big giant of *commitment*.

Have you ever felt that you were not quite far enough to reach the other side, but you have also gone too far to turn back? This is what transpires with many people. They get halfway to Jericho, but then want to go back. They say, "This is too tough—it is too hard!" and they decide to drop out and camp out at a town called 'Comfort.'

Others keep going, all the way through the wilderness, and pass the first test. But when they reach Jericho, the point of no return, they realize how much that their own personal agenda has been decreasing. And rather than crossing over into total self-abandonment, they stop and say, "I can't afford to decrease anymore. I can't give anymore. I have been serving for so long; now it's time for *me* to *be served*. I'm sure I have already learned enough. I don't have to keep serving someone else." So they settle in places called 'Religion,' 'Self-Promotion,' and 'Professional Phoniness.'

But only a few are like Elisha. After all was said and done, there was only one follower that Elijah just couldn't get rid of. He was the one that just kept saying, "As surely as the Lord lives, and you yourself live, I will never leave you!"

"Why don't you just leave me alone? Why don't you just go away like all the rest?"

"No, I'm not giving up," Elisha insisted. "I'm not quitting. I'm not going anywhere."[8]

Remember, a taker is interested in the blessing, but the giver is interested in the

> WINNERS MAKE DECISIONS WHICH PREPARE THEM FOR THE FUTURE THEY HAVE BEEN PROMISED. LOSERS CELEBRATE THE DECISIONS THAT BRING THEM MOMENTARY SATISFACTION.

---

8. See 2 Kings 2, author's paraphrase

inheritance. I will put off my present pleasure. I will endure the pain of today, to enjoy the pleasure of tomorrow. I will give up *short-term gratification* in order to inherit *long-term greatness.*

Endurance, in the face of hardship develops strength of character in us. Character strengthens our confident expectation, and this expectation *will not disappoint us.* We must covenant with those who have shown that they will never give up. Together, *we will win,* if we just do not quit!

REWARDS GO TO OVERCOMERS

Everyone has to come to his or her exam time in life. We can't just continually go to school and never take finals. It may take you five years to get to the test you must pass, in order to be promoted. And no matter how long it takes to get there, do you realize that 100% of your grade is based on whether you pass that final or not? You'll never go beyond the test that you fail.

After failing a test, many people start blaming others, instead of examining their own mistakes. They start pointing fingers, saying, "They're just holding me back—they don't understand; they don't know what I've been through, and they don't really care." Then, they unhook and move to a smaller league, where the tests are not as difficult.

> THE REWARDS OF LIFE ARRIVE ONLY UPON THE DOORSTEPS OF THE OVERCOMERS.

But what these people don't realize is that the rewards of life do not happen for everyone. Most people that you know, truthfully, are losing in life, because they are content with surviving, rather than overcoming. But, *the rewards of life arrive only upon the doorsteps of the overcomers.*

David's reward for slaying Goliath was much greater than his reward for killing the lion or the bear. Your reward is determined by the size of the giants you are able *to slay.* You may be *remembered* for the giants that you are willing to face, but you'll only be *rewarded* for the giants that you *overcome*. It is the overcomer who has moved from mediocrity to excellence, for the only difference between mediocrity and excellence is *completion*.

To the American reader, here is something for you to ponder. The poorest person inside our nation is better off than almost ninety percent of the rest of the world's population. Most of us don't realize that even in the midst of our difficulties, we are better off than people that live affluently in other parts of the earth. Because we do not understand how fortunate we are, ingratitude begins to rumble from the bottom, and spill out into every area of life. Consequently, we begin to think that privileges are *owed* to us; thus, we put pressure on our government to give us more. Instead of overcoming our personal giants of poor choice and selfishness, the government becomes our god, and the only thing we have to show for our lives is a long list of good intentions. And remember—it is impossible to be promoted for *intention*, because promotion is the reward for *productivity*.

> IT IS IMPOSSIBLE TO BE PROMOTED FOR *INTENTION*, BECAUSE PROMOTION IS THE REWARD FOR *PRODUCTIVITY*.

Never get caught in the trap of knowing too much and doing too little. If you are not *doing* what you are thinking, then eject what you are thinking! The rewards of life come only to the walkers, not to the talkers. You need to go back and look at your life and see what you have *done*. Don't look at what you *say*, look at what you've *done* because what you've done is what you really believe.

Friend, quit listening to people's words and watch their feet. If you just watch their feet and what they do, you will know who they are.

Being an overcomer is an "inside job." Success exists *internally* long before it manifests on the outside of a person. Ascendancy on the exterior of an individual's life is an indication that winning has been the abundance of his or her heart for quite some time. We are deceiving ourselves to think that we can overcome outward obstacles, if we are still satisfied with mediocrity, neutrality, and compromise in our inner man.

Read with me these powerful words written to the Hebrews:

> **Our great desire is that you will keep right on loving others as long as life lasts, in order to make certain that what you hope for will come true. Then you will not become spiritually dull and indifferent. Instead, you will follow the example of those who are going to inherit God's promises because of their faith and patience.**[9]

Paul's admonition made it clear that the fulfillment of their own personal hopes and aspirations hinged directly on their ability to love others. He also indicated that nurturing those relationships would prevent them from becoming "spiritually dull and indifferent." The Greek word for this phrase is *nothros*. It gives us the picture of someone who has sunk into a state of being *sluggish, slow, monotonous, and uninterested; something that has lost its speed or momentum.* They were still moving, but not with the same velocity or aggressiveness they once had. They had lost the drive, thrust, impetus, pace, and speed they had once possessed. This word portrays the image of someone who has lost his intense zeal and conviction about a matter that was once of great importance to him.[10]

An overcomer does not allow a "middle-of-the-road" attitude or a "take-it-or-leave-it" mentality to remain in his heart. He knows such thoughts are barriers to his advancement and death to all his dreams. Instead, he throws off neutrality, ejects indifference, and engages, full throttle, into the passionate pursuit of winning. He is determined to obtain an overcomer's reward and to bring honor to those who have believed in him and fathered him.

HONORING FATHERS

The deep desire of a true son is to add *honor* to his father. Honor is the willingness to acknowledge what someone has done, while ignoring what they have not. A true son adds honor in *every* way, not just in the gifts he sows. He adds

---

9. Hebrews 6:11-12, *NLT*
10. Rick Renner, *Sparkling Gems from the Greek* (Tulsa, OK: Teach All Nations, 2003), p. 133.

honor with words. He adds honor through protection. He adds honor by build-ing what belongs to the father, for he knows that, *"Until you are faithful in that which is another man's, God will not give you what is your own."*[11]

The word "honor" is derived from the Greek word *timao,* which portrays the idea of *something so valuable that it is held as precious, prized, cherished, esteemed, treasured, and very dear.*[12] To "give honor" refers to *a purposeful, premeditated, and calculated decision to intentionally demon-strate attention, consideration, appreciation, and respect* for someone.[13]

> HONOR
>
> IS THE WILLINGNESS
>
> TO ACKNOWLEDGE
>
> WHAT SOMEONE HAS DONE,
>
> WHILE IGNORING
>
> WHAT THEY HAVE NOT.

God intended the fathers in our lives to be esteemed, respected, and cherished in a very purposeful and premeditated fashion. The relationship between a father and son is far too valuable and precious to ever be treated in an off-handed or haphazard manner. It must be handled with the utmost reverence.

We see the cherished value of the father/son relationship, as we take one last look at the story of Elijah and Elisha. The day came when the angels of God came down in the whirlwind and separated Elijah and Elisha. And as Elijah was taken up in the whirlwind, Elisha cried out, "My Father, My Father!"

He didn't cry out, "Praise the Lord, I got my wish, thank you God, I got my wish, I'm just so happy, because now it's my turn!" No! He cried *for his father,* because *his relationship with his father meant more to him than his own future and being able to establish himself.*

Once I began to understand these things, relationships became much more precious to me. I began to learn how to walk with my fathers and truly honor them.

We have grown up in a society where we have to reinvent the wheel every gen-eration, because we shamelessly disrespect and reject our seniors, thinking that they know nothing. Do you understand what an old person is? *They're just a young person with time on them.* They're just a young person who has the advantage of

---

11. Luke 16: 12, author's paraphrase
12. James Strong, *The New Strong's Exhaustive Concordance of the Bible/Dictionary of the Greek Testament* (Nashville, TN: Thomas Nelson Publishers, 1990) p. 506/72.
13. Ibid, p. 403/14.

wisdom and experience; that's all an old person is.

You may hear older people make comments like, "I scare myself when I look in the mirror. I don't know what's happening to me on the outside, but on the inside, I don't feel any different than I've ever felt. But, I have noticed I just don't have the drive that I once had. Certain things don't really matter to me like they use to. Even though I'm a person of excellence, I'm not really trying to push toward it anymore, because there's hardly anyone to be excellent for. Very few people appreciate it or understand it, and fewer still are willing to follow."

Whether in the natural or spiritual realm, each and every one of us wants to pour our life into someone who will *truly follow*. Jesus said, "*...If ye continue in My Word, then are ye My disciples indeed, and ye shall know the truth and the truth shall make you free.*"[14] Now, I would say that over ninety-eight percent of people *do not continue*. They get to a place in their life where they feel that they've actually arrived, and they no longer need to posture as a student. They forget that it takes the same amount of courage to sit down and listen as it does to stand up and speak!

> IT TAKES THE SAME AMOUNT OF COURAGE TO SIT DOWN AND LISTEN AS IT DOES TO STAND UP AND SPEAK.

One of the things that I've recognized as being extremely important is being able to *continue* in relationship *after having matured*. One must learn how to continue to posture as a son, long after he, himself, has become a father. He is a wise man who still knows how to be a son, even when he's seventy years old. A man of protocol continually asks himself, "Have I become an honorable representative of the precious deposit that was placed inside me by my fathers?"

Your life is determined by how hard you are willing to press. The harder that you press, the farther you'll go. So, you must look for and *follow* the coaches and the fathers in your life. You must follow someone who is going to provoke and incite you, saying, "Come on, keep pressing. Let us find out if you've got what it takes. Let's find out if you are still going to be a son."

---

14. John 8: 31-32, *KJV*

Every father will give an account to God for the sons and daughters he has fathered. The highest form of honor that a son can give his father is to have *truly followed*. For then, the father can give an account with joy, and not with grief.[15] The cry of every father's heart is, *"Son, be wise, so that I can answer my critics."*[16]

The anointed fathers of your life are qualified to be your connection to change. *Your response to a man of God determines Heaven's response to you.* What you respect is what increases in your life. Stay very sensitive to respecting and honoring your

> YOUR RESPONSE TO A MAN OF GOD DETERMINES HEAVEN'S RESPONSE TO YOU.

fathers. Look for opportunities to express that respect and honor, for *before honor can become a harvest in your life, it must first be your seed.* Grasp and live this concept, and you will be operating at the highest levels of the Law of Ascent.

---

15. See Hebrews 13:17
16. Proverbs 27:11, *NIV*, author's paraphrase

THE LAW OF ASCENT

Walk with the great, and you will become great.

+ In order to get close to greatness, I must comply with greatness.
+ Consequences are the detentions you receive when you refuse to sit at the feet of an instructor.
+ Wisdom is the reward provided for those who walk in humility.
+ The bastard is only interested in the blessing of the father; the son is interested in the inheritance of his father.
+ Your posture will determine your ascent.
+ You will be both blessed by the virtues and cursed by the vices of those closest to you.
+ A man is not defined by his beliefs, but by the quality of his actions.
+ Your character is the foundation upon which your life's work is built.
+ Today's excellence is tomorrow's mediocrity.
+ It is impossible to correct what you are unwilling to face.
+ It is impossible for your life to produce anything beyond the strength of your moral fiber.
+ Mediocrity pursues comfort, while excellence pursues change.
+ Submission to authority is the avenue through which my character is developed.
+ With every promotion comes greater responsibility.
+ Greatness becomes yours the moment you become small in your own eyes.
+ Winners make decisions which prepare them for the future they have been promised. Losers celebrate the decisions that bring them momentary satisfaction.
+ The rewards of life arrive only upon the doorsteps of the overcomers.

→ **It is impossible to be promoted for your intentions, because promotion is the reward for productivity.**

→ **Honor is the willingness to acknowledge what someone has done, while ignoring what they have not.**

→ **It takes the same amount of courage to sit down and listen as it does to stand up and speak.**

→ **Your response to a man of God determines Heaven's response to you.**

Conclusion

THE POWER OF PARADOX

These Ten Critical Laws of Relationship reveal the power of paradox in God's kingdom. As the world screams that self-promotion is your only path to success, the voice of wisdom whispers that to be lifted up, you must bow down. To find greatness, you must embrace humility. To be worthy of being served, you must first sacrificially serve others.

The Father's heart tells you that the road to the throne goes through the altar, and if you want to win, you must surrender. To be made whole, you must be bruised, and to be perfected, you must bear scars. To be made strong, you must glory in your weakness, and to be honored, you must be abased. Your life is forever changed when you discover that to increase, you must decrease, and to truly live, you must first die.

There is a seed of greatness planted in the heart of every man, woman, boy, and girl. There is a God-ordained destiny and purpose written for each one of us to fulfill. *The secret key to that destiny is wrapped up in our relationships.*

The seed you hold in your hand today is enough to generate the future you crave. The only ingredient as important as good seed is good ground. Even the best seed cannot change the quality of the ground. The relationships you pursue become the soil for your seed. Those relationships will enhance your life, or they will choke the seed and bring barrenness. The harvest you end up with will be largely determined by the soil of your relationships—so choose your relationships wisely!

I strongly suggest that you read this book several times, until you firmly grasp these laws. Behind these critical laws is the secret to building your future and to inheriting your God-given purpose.